DATE DUE

PROJECTIVE METHODS

Publication Number 10

AMERICAN LECTURE SERIES

A Monograph In

AMERICAN LECTURES IN PSYCHOLOGY

Edited by
Molly Harrower, Ph.D.
Research and Consulting Psychologist,
New York City
Formerly Clinical Psychologist, Montreal
Neurological Institute, McGill University,
Montreal, Canada

PROJECTIVE METHODS

by

LAWRENCE K. FRANK

Director, Zachry Institute of Human Development
New York City

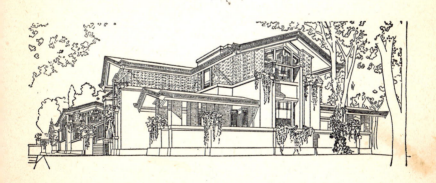

CHARLES C THOMAS · PUBLISHER
Springfield · Illinois · U.S.A.

CHARLES C THOMAS · PUBLISHER
BANNERSTONE HOUSE
301-327 East Lawrence Avenue, Springfield, Illinois

Published simultaneously in The British Commonwealth of Nations by
BLACKWELL SCIENTIFIC PUBLICATIONS, LTD., OXFORD, ENGLAND

Published simultaneously in Canada by
THE RYERSON PRESS, TORONTO

Copyright, 1948, by CHARLES C THOMAS · PUBLISHER

First Edition

Printed in the United States of America

137. 8
7 85p

PREFACE

THIS lecture offers an introduction to the place, significance and underlying theory of projective methods in psychology, their relation to recent developments in scientific thinking and methodology and a brief description of the different kinds of projective procedures now in use. The lecture does not give any specific direction for using or interpreting projective results but rather provides what may be called the rationale of such methods.

PLAN

The first part discusses the growing use of projective methods in psychology and psychiatry and shows how they are predicated upon a psychocultural conception of the emergence of the personality and its dynamic operation.

The second part describes recent developments in scientific concepts and methods, especially in physics and chemistry and medicine, as illustrative of the new climate of opinion we are now entering.

The third part reviews various approaches to the study and diagnosis of personality by way of preface to the more specific description of actual procedures.

The fourth part outlines projective techniques and describes the five different varieties thus far developed, with interpretative comment upon the value and use of each variety.

The fifth part discusses reliability and validity of projective methods and the emergence of new criteria for assaying projective procedures.

PURPOSE

This monograph has been prepared to direct the attention of students toward recent developments in scientific thinking which have revolutionized physical science and offer immense possibilities for advancing psychology as soon as these new concepts and assumptions are understood and the new criteria and methodologies are accepted by psychologists. It is hoped that a reading of this lecture in print will stimulate further "explorations in personality" and also enlist a wider public awareness of what is taking place today in study and diagnosis of personality.

Finally, this monograph is offered as a contribution to the further development of mental hygiene in education, industry and public administration by showing how better personnel selection may be achieved through the use of projective methods.

L. K. F.

New York City

CONTENTS

PROJECTIVE METHODS

I

PROJECTIVE METHODS

THE growing interest in and use of projective techniques for the study, diagnosis and treatment of personality are indicative of a number of significant developments in our social life and in the professional practices of psychotherapists. They also reflect the changing climate of opinion coming with recent developments in scientific concepts and techniques.

THE SOCIAL SITUATION

It has become evident that as a people we are exhibiting many forms of personality difficulties, as dramatically shown by the frequency of rejections by the Selective Service and of discharges from the armed forces, for various personality disorders. Likewise, the increasing demands upon the relatively limited number of clinics for diagnosis and treatment of children, adolescents and adults suffering from various personality maladjustments, behavior problems, emotional disturbances or engaged in anti-social acts, indicate the growing extent, both of personality difficulties and of public reliance upon these clinical agencies for assistance.

The small number of psychiatrists and psychoanalysts is unable to meet the demand for individual diagnoses and treatment of the large numbers in need of such care. Accordingly, there are many explorations into shorter forms of psychotherapy, including narcotherapy and hypnotherapy, and the use of group therapy and the development of counseling and guidance services.

What is also significant is the growing reliance, of psychotherapists and others engaged in counseling, upon various tests and procedures to provide a diagnosis, or at least to give some initial understanding, of the character-structure and personality makeup, especially the emotional or affective reactions, of the individuals whom they are preparing to diagnose or treat, advise or counsel.

Until recently the psychotherapist was like the physician of a generation or so ago who was compelled to make a diagnosis on the basis of his personal observation and external examination of the patient. With the development of the modern medical laboratory and the growing number of laboratory tests and procedures, the physician can now obtain a comprehensive evaluation of the patient's anatomy, physiology and various specific reactions, for making a differential diagnosis and for evaluating his treatment.

The medical laboratory has not in any way rendered unnecessary the clinical judgment of the physician; it provides a variety of data upon the individual patient which the physician can use in making his initial diagnosis and for directing the therapy he may apply. But it must be emphasized that each of the most objective, quantitative findings of the medical laboratory must be related to all other findings and evaluated and interpreted by the physician in terms of the individual patient, his or her age, sex, occupation, previous illnesses and other significant aspects of his history and previous experience, with his current condition or complaint. These quantitative laboratory reports are, therefore, subject to clinical judgment by the physician who will give each of them a relative weight and meaning according to each patient as they are combined into a diagnosis. This is the method of biological relativity which orders every observation or measurement to the field (organism-personality) of its occurrence.

The development of psychological tests and procedures for evaluating the personality may be viewed as a parallel development with laboratory procedures in internal medicine. These new procedures are beginning to provide the psychotherapist with basic data about the individual, with which he can make a clinical diagnosis for guiding his treatment. They are also providing methods for evaluating treatment and, in some cases, are of direct use as therapy (just as x-rays may be used for diagnosis, for evaluating treatment and as a form of therapy).

This development of personality tests and procedures, as a parallel or equivalent to the medical laboratory, carries a number of implications which should be clearly recognized. It seems evident that *no matter how objective or quantitative a test may be, the use of the findings will call for clinical experience and judgment in the field of personality development and/or psychotherapy.* Moreover, it indicates that increasingly psychotherapists and indeed all those engaged in counseling, guiding and advising individuals, will turn to the psychological laboratory for an initial evaluation and diagnosis of the personality and for aid in treatment or guidance. As schools, including nursery schools, and colleges become more aware of the need for educational therapy, they will increasingly call for the assistance of the well trained psychological examiner, skilled in the use and interpretation of personality tests and procedures, with an adequate background of clinical training.

The Changing Climate of Opinion

Concurrently with these developments in our social life and in our diagnostic procedures, there has been a significant development in American psychology, of an interest in the underlying concepts and basic assumptions of the investigator. More and more one finds in the journals rather elaborate statements of the assumptions and of the conceptual formulations which have been employed by the investigator to collect and order his data and give them meaning. This marks a growing sophistication as contrasted with the earlier preoccupation with methodologies and the presentation of data as the sole concern of scientific study.

This departure from the sometimes naïve empiricism of earlier days and from the timid, apologetic theorizing that "explained" the findings, is fostering a critical awareness of the significance of concepts and of the persistence of obsolete concepts. Also, a greater readiness to recognize cultural patterns and other procedures is being revealed.[1]

In the field of personality studies, such critical awareness is being recognized as essential to guard against the many archaic assumptions that still survive from the earlier, animistic tradition of a psychic entity and the still prevalent dualistic beliefs about human nature and human behavior (mind versus body). Likewise, this awareness is helping us to escape from some of the assumptions of *ad hoc* forces (such as special motives) and psychic entities (traits) which were displaced long ago in physics (by Gallilei's conception of inertia), but still linger in the social sciences, especially in psychology.

---

[1] Cf. Edward C. Tolman, A Stimulus-Expectancy Need-Cathexis Psychology, *Science*, Vol. 101, No. 2616. February 16, 1945.

Because of this growing concern with concepts and theory, one need not today apologize for offering a conceptual statement in the discussion of a scientific problem or a methodology. Indeed, it may be said that during this current period of transition, an investigator is under obligation to declare his preconceptions so that the reader can initially decide how relevant any study may be to the ongoing development of scientific investigation. Many a careful, detailed study is obsolete before the investigator has made his first observations because it is directed by obsolete assumptions and utilizes out-of-date conceptions of the problem for which no methodological or quantitative precision will compensate.

Indeed, one may say that the investigator's assumptions and his initial conceptions operate to govern his thinking and focus his observations *selectively* so that he will formulate his problem and will choose or devise his methodology and collect his data according to what he theoretically expects to find and will interpret his findings according to the way he has conceived the order of events. As Carrel pointed out some years ago:

In the development of every science, the conception is more important than the method. Techniques are only the servants of ideas. A method is an instrument which finds only that which is being sought.[2]

Sometimes the investigator who has developed skill in the use of a special technique will develop or choose his conceptions to bring a problem within reach of his methodologies (as, for example, the attempt to reduce all problems to the relation of two variables, or the discovery of a few factors, to be studied statistically).

In the light of the foregoing, it is scarcely necessary to ask indulgence for offering an initial statement about the emergence of personality, to indicate, if not define, the conception of the personality which underlies the various tests and procedures called *projective techniques*. The personality must be approached in new terms, conceived as emerging from prior experiences in a cultural field, and operating as a dynamic process, if projective techniques are to become meaningful and valid.

The relation of this dynamic conception and of these techniques

[2] "The New Cytology," *Science*, 73: 1890, 298, 1931.

to recent scientific developments can then be discussed as a preface to the examination of various projective techniques.

THE PSYCHOCULTURAL APPROACH

Utilizing the findings and insights of psychiatry and psychology, together with the concepts and understandings contributed by cultural anthropology, we may approach the personality as emerging from the culturizing and socializing of the child who takes over and accepts cultural patterns and social practices, but always in his own idiomatic fashion.

We thereby face two problems for study: *the generalized process of personality development and the emergence of the more or less unique individualized personality, to be revealed by projective methods.* To gain an insightful understanding of these personality problems, we need a larger and deeper perspective which may be briefly sketched in the following.

Everywhere, all over the world, the geographical environment that we call nature, is essentially alike. While there are local differences in topography, in climate and weather, with different plants and animals in each area, the basic processes we call physical, chemical and biological are regular, orderly and unchanging. Nature is everywhere similar.

Moreover, the various members of the human race are essentially alike. While differing in size, color and some physiological capacities, man, the genus *homo*, is basically similar, sharing the same mammalian ancestry, with the same organic functions and needs. Man everywhere is essentially alike.

But despite this regularity of nature and similarity of man, different groups of people are found all over the earth pursuing different goals and values and maintaining different designs for living, each group living in a symbolic, cultural world which it has created and imposed upon nature and human nature. Nowhere do we find man existing like other organisms, on the level of physiological functioning and organic impulse.

Each species has developed a way of existence, a way of utilizing the environment selectively to meet its specialized needs and to provide for its differentiated organic capacities. Thus, in the same life space we find bacteria, insects, reptiles, fish, birds and mammals, each finding sustenance and achieving survival in one of the many "worlds" which that common geographical environment provides for their specialized use.

But man, instead of adapting himself to the environment like other organisms, has established a human way of life. Unlike all other organisms which developed a specialized, differentiated organism for a specific life zone, man has remained plastic and undifferentiated, by relying upon ideas, weapons and tools for creating his own human way of living. Man, therefore, has established his many different cultural worlds by selectively utilizing the environment of nature and selectively developing, elaborating and rejecting the various capacities and potentialities of human nature, according to his ideas and conceptions and his feelings.

Man, as an organism, therefore *exists* in the geographical environment of nature where he is exposed to the impact of physical, chemical and biological processes. As a member of a group he carries on his life activities in the cultural world of his traditions and in the social world of his historically developed institutions, laws and approved practices. But as an individual personality he *lives* in a "private world" of his own, created and imposed upon the geographical environment, the cultural and social world, according to what he individually has learned and how he has felt.

We may, therefore, look upon the personality as a dynamic process, the continual activity of the individual who is engaged in creating, maintaining and defending that "private world" wherein he lives.

How the individual personality emerges is to be seen as a sequential process of growth, development and maturation during which the young mammalian organism is progressively transformed into a participating member of his group. In accordance with his inherited constitution and capacities, he will learn to transform his biological hunger into the patterned appetite for the kind of food, eaten at intervals favored by his group. Also, he will learn to manage his elimination, regulating and controlling these automatic functions to conform to the requirements, simple or elaborate, of his group with certain practices of cleanliness, sanitation and modesty or shame. Moreover, he will in greater or less measure learn to curb the all-over physiological disturbance we call emotional reactions, limiting their occurrence according to what his family permit or encourage and utilizing whatever form of expression, overt or disguised, he has found to be necessary or congenial.

The infant mammalian organism is thus compelled to surrender his physiological autonomy, to accept the regulation and control of his functional processes and thereby incorporate the approved patterns of his family and the group traditions into the internal world of his developing organism-personality.

Moreover, the child, as soon as he begins to move about and explore the world, meets the many prohibitions against touching, taking, eating or otherwise approaching the objects and animals and the places that are prohibited to him or considered dangerous. He also must learn to refrain from attacking other individuals and to respect their bodily integrity. Through these lessons, involving continual denials and frustrations, the growing child learns to observe the inviolabilities of things we call private property or the sacredness of places and the personal rights of persons.

The young child likewise is expected to accept the many prescribed patterns and practices for personal living (e.g., grooming and cleanliness), for interpersonal relations, such as manners and etiquette, and other formalities of approach, the early expression of masculine or feminine rôles and other required ways of acting and performing what is required.

Through these lessons the growing child learns to live in a world defined by the parents, who indicate not only what he must *not* do, must do and may do, but by various methods persuade or coerce him into accepting these definitions and performing these prescribed actions.

From this parental teaching the child learns to transform his naïve, impulsive behavior into patterned conduct addressed to situations and people as they have been defined by adults. He may react to this frustration, coercion, and punishment with the emotional reaction we call anger, rage or fear. Thus, he learns these various patterns of conduct in his own individualized way of conforming and with the feelings that they have aroused during such learning.

When the individual is exposed to frequent or continual provocations to emotional reactions which he cannot escape or meet effectively, he may develop chronic affective reactions; anger and rage become hostility, fear becomes anxiety and guilt, which he then carries in his organism as a pervasive set or physiological state, localized in one or more organ systems or functional processes (such as digestion or elimination, breathing or heart and circulation). Thereby, he can carry on various activities and functions necessary to life, such as eating, sleeping and motor activities but at the same time maintain these persistent affective reactions in his organism.

What is of special significance is that *the child's internal environment of physiological functions becomes organized and patterned under this parental care and treatment.* He develops his individualized way of functioning to meet parental demands and restrictions and of reacting emotionally to such experiences. Moreover, he develops his own peculiar way of feeling toward his parents and the world, largely as his internal world functions, including these emotional or chronic affective reactions.

Thus, it appears that if the baby is fed whenever hungry, he gets more than food: he is protected from the tension or pain of unrelieved hunger and so learns to expect such care and to rely upon parental treatment. He thereby develops confidence in the world and begins to trust people, as contrasted with the infant who has been subjected to prolonged hunger and neglect or maltreatment.

Likewise, if allowed to eliminate freely until ready to assume this first responsibility for managing his own organic functions, he will develop an internal world without the strains and tensions that premature toilet training may establish.

The kind of emotional reactions he has experienced also enter into the organization of his internal environment. If the child has been guarded from unnecessary denials and compulsions and has been protected from too frequent emotional disturbances, he will develop more and more stability in his internal environment and be more and more capable of tolerating the situations that earlier aroused his anger or fear. Toward his parents he will, if treated with tenderness and given warm, cherishing care and love, begin to give love and affection.

When exposed to continual frustration and coercion and frequently provoked emotionally, he may reluctantly accept the prohibitions and compulsions and develop anxiety or hostility, becoming docile and submissive or aggressively destructive.

The child is expected to take over these lessons, incorporate them into his own conduct so that he will learn to impose these prohibitions upon himself as self-administered inhibitions. Likewise, he must learn to observe the prescribed patterns of action, directing himself to perform, whenever appropriate, what he was earlier compelled to do. In this way the requirements of social life are established in the growing child but each child will conform in his own individualized way, utilizing the socially sanctioned patterns but always doing so in his peculiar personal interpretation and application.

Moreover, in all that he does his conduct is colored by his persistent feelings, derived from the earlier experiences in which he learned those patterns. Every learned pattern of conduct is accompained by feelings, just as every patterned functional activity is accompanied by feelings.

The child is thus inducted into the culturally defined and socially patterned group life, expected to conform sufficiently to make his conduct acceptable and understandable to others, but permitted to do so with such variations and deviations as do not conflict with the parental and group norms of conduct.

All these lessons serve to pattern the child's behavior into the approved patterns of conduct. But he is not completely absorbed into the cultural world of his family and group traditions until he begins to use language and to accept the names, symbols and concepts, the customary reasons, explanations and sanctions, given by the parents for what they do and for whatever exists and happens.

With language the child begins to respond to verbal symbols as surrogates for the parental hand. He learns to do and to refrain from doing as directed by mother's voice and to accept her verbal reassurances or her scoldings in place of physical contacts and punishment. He becomes increasingly sensitized to words and sentences and the intonations that convey approval or disapproval, or otherwise arouse his feelings.

Then he is given the names or verbal symbols for every object, animal, situation, person, activity and relation, whereby he learns to see everything around him in terms of the meaning and significance of these verbalized definitions. Progressively he is inculcated with the ideas, the assumptions, the organizing conceptions of his cultural traditions which transform the geographical environment and all it contains into the symbolic, cultural world in which he must learn to live.

There is an endless dialogue between the inquiring child, asking questions, and the parents, answering in terms of their religion, their philosophy, their moral, ethical and legal principles, their cherished myths and folklore and such scientific knowledge as they may have accepted. Thus, the child learns to organize all his experience, to build up the concepts with expectations and assumptions which constitute the symbolic cultural world of human living.

While there is a more or less clearly formulated statement of these beliefs and assumptions in the creeds of churches and in the books of philosophy and law, each family has its own version of these derived from its regional and rural or urban origin, its social-economic class status, its formal education, its sectarian religious allegiances, etc.

Moreover, each parent, being a unique personality with a life history, will of necessity communicate these ideas and explanations in a more or less biased, even distorted, version. Thus, what the parents tell the child is rarely or ever complete or symmetrical and is usually warped by the parental feelings toward specific points in these traditions upon which they had difficulties in their childhood or youth.

In telling the child these highly individualized versions of what he is to believe and how he is to think, the parents may further distort their teachings by their personal feelings toward the individual child whom they have loved or rejected. Moreover, they often communicate some of the more crucial ideas under emotional tension, as when the child has transgressed their code or when the child or parent is stirred by feelings of awe or anxiety or guilt.

What the parents attempt to teach the child is, therefore, often far removed from the standardized formulation of the cultural traditions. Moreover, the child will learn from this teaching what it means to him and how he feels toward the parents and the ideas they are expressing.

Usually the child's limited understanding of language, his restricted, childish comprehension and his misinterpretation of what he hears, according to his already established beliefs and feelings, operate to establish his unique constellation of ideas, beliefs, misconceptions, partial understandings, with many gaps and overelaborations and distortions.

This curious personalized version of cultural traditions the child sets up as his personal frame of reference, his individualized way of organizing and interpreting all experience, of creating and maintaining the symbolic world of meanings and values, of assumptions and expectations, that he must impose upon all situations and events and people and himself, as a member of his cultural group.

From his parents' words the child begins to form an image of the self as loved and wanted or hated and rejected, as good or bad, as unworthy or worthy. Moreover, as the child experiences the parental authority, mainly prohibitions and compulsions, he often develops a persistent way of feeling and acting toward authority, with patterns or aggressive hostility or submissive obedience.

Out of these experiences the child establishes his image, his personal expectations and level of aspirations as he not only observes the property and rights of others and performs prescribed practices but also maintains (or fails to maintain) his own property and rights against others as he accepts or rejects their approaches.

It must be emphasized again and again that man as an organism exists in the geographical world of nature, but he lives in the human world of his cultural traditions that is maintained by this learned way of investing the world and people with these tradi-

tional meanings and imputed relations as he interprets them and feels toward them.

Man lives by his beliefs and ideas, his memories and expectations, and his feelings. Each individual of necessity does this in his own individualized way. Moreover, since ideas are plastic and flexible, easily manipulated and combined with images (visual and other sensory), each individual can and does create a personal symbolic world which differs from that of others. Within his private world he may fantasy whatever he feels or desires, often finding in these ideas and images a more congenial place than the frequently refractory and frustrating world of group living. Moreover, he can explain everything to himself according to his feelings.

In his reveries and fantasies each individual continually talks to himself, as he rehearses in his own personal way, what he has been taught in childhood to believe and do and *not* do, as essential to social living—to live according to ideas and patterns and feelings, channelling all his impulses and emotions and his naïve behavior into the traditional forms and patterns of his family and group traditions.

Since this basic transformation takes place early in life when the infant and young child are plastic and flexible, still physiologically uncoördinated and unskilled, before they have developed much language, these parental teachings and training are built into the developing organism. The child learns, therefore, to function internally and to act externally as prescribed by his parents as the only way that is permitted or is effective for conducting human relations. Moreover, he learns to believe and to think as he has been inculcated by the cultural traditions. But in all these he develops his individualized version of these patterns, reacting with emotions or feelings of his persistent affective reactions. Once these patterns and feelings are established, they will persist unless and until some event of sufficient intensity changes them or the individual is helped to change. The child's private frame of reference ordinarily does not alter except when specially reëducated for a profession or by intensive psychotherapy.

Thus, in each individual there is a "forgotten childhood," the patterns established in childhood which became the basis for all subsequent learning and living, giving the individual his peculiar, personal orientation to every situation and person, his idiomatic way of thinking, acting and feeling. In adolescence the individual undergoes a series of experiences which further fixate his childhood patterns or sometimes modify them depending upon what he or she meets in the teen-age period.

The personality then may be viewed as this dynamic process of establishing and maintaining and defending the individual's private world. It is the same creative activity expressed by man's setting up and perpetuating his cultural world but each personality always organizes and interprets experience according to what he, as an individual personality, has selectively accepted and rejected and utilized and felt. Within this private world the personality carries on the drama of his life as it revolves around his image of himself, however that may be conceived by the individual, with all others playing the rôles he imposes upon them in his private world.

Needless to say, by the very process of personality development, with the child subjected to the care and rearing, the authority and control of individual parental personalities, almost every conceivable kind of personality can and does emerge from these childhood experiences. Each will of necessity reflect and utilize the traditional patterns, exhibiting the generalized or modal patterns of thinking, acting and feeling that maintain social order and likewise form the character-structure of a people. But each will use these in a different way and in unique configurations, as shown by his or her own conduct and ideas and expectations.

What is of major significance for understanding the individual personality is that the individual organizes experience as he warps, twists, distorts and otherwise fits every situation, event and person into the framework of his private world, giving them the affective significance which they must have for him in his private world. Moreover, the individual may attempt to impose his personal beliefs and feelings upon the world of people and events or carefully guard his private world from any public disclosure that might reveal his own ideas and feelings.

Each personality tried to maintain his or her private world by imposing upon situation and people whatever they mean to him or her. Thereby, each individual *creates* his own personality problems which he attempts to meet or to resolve by the same ideas and conduct which create those problems. Thus we see a circular process—often self-defeating—at work in the individual personality, who is usually unable to extricate himself from these difficulties without help from someone.

If personality is conceived as emerging from early life experience, the problem of personality may be formulated in terms of the dynamic processes described above. The task of understanding any individual personality is thus seen as a problem of discovering how the individual utilizes these dynamic processes to produce the differentiated outcomes or products we observe in his speech, conduct and beliefs and feelings and functional processes.

These problems call for methods and techniques which are appropriate for revealing patterns and persistent configurations and for investigating *processes*, as contrasted with the description, classification, cataloging and measuring of *products*. For promising leads to the study of processes, we may take note of what has developed within the past four or five decades in the physical sciences which are now concerned more and more with dynamic problems, of revealing the basic processes underlying physical and chemical events.

II

RECENT SCIENTIFIC DEVELOPMENTS

DURING the past fifty years there has been a truly revolutionary development in physical science, bringing a new climate of opinion, with new assumptions and organizing conceptions, new methodologies and new criteria of credibility. These all have a significance for the life sciences, especially for psychology, which has been following, as closely as it could manage, the concepts and methods of classical physics but now must enlarge and adapt its thinking and procedures to these new ideas and methods.

In the field of personality study and diagnosis, these recent scientific developments offer promising leads to problems that have long been elusive. They also provide a rationale and a sanction for the procedures employed in projective technique.

Until recently scientific thinking has been primarily concerned with the discovery of regularities and uniformities, to be formulated in terms of laws and generalizations. There has been a recognition that these observed regularities arise from the activities of many anonymous individual events, each of which is erratic, disorderly and individually unpredictable but, as an aggregate, they exhibit a statistical regularity and order. Scientific thinking and investigation today are being focussed more and more upon the study of identified units and the dynamic processes which underlie these statistical regularities.

As Irving Langmuir has stated it, classical physics was concerned with the convergent events which exhibit a statistical regularity but recent physical theories are concerned with divergent events:

We must recognize two types of natural phenomena. *First*, that in which the behavior of the system can be determined from the average behavior of its component parts and, *second*, those in which a single discontinuous event (which may depend upon a single quantum change) becomes magnified in its effect so that the behavior of the whole aggregate does depend upon something that started from a small beginning. The first class of phenomena I want to call *convergent* phenomena, because all the fluctuating details of the individual atoms average out, giving a result that converges to a definite state. The second class we call *divergent phenomena*, where from a small beginning increasingly large effects are produced. In general then we may say that classical physics applies satisfactorily to convergent phenomena and that they conform well to the older ideas of cause and effect. The divergent phenomena on the other hand can best be understood on the basis of quantum theory of modern physics. (pp. 3-4)[1]

This is significant as indicating how physical theory today is moving from its former preoccupation with quantitative studies of large scale statistical regularities and orderliness, to a concern with the problem of the single individual event which occurs in discontinuous sequences and as a specific quantum. Classical physics was concerned with mass events, as in thermodynamics and statistical mechanics, where it was neither necessary nor possible to identify any single event, hence the study of the average behavior of an aggregate of events or particles (or molecules).[2] The newer approach of quantum physics recognizes that each individual emission and absorption of energy is a single event (which cannot always be identified) but can be conceived theoretically as an identifiable event subject to probability calculation and, under certain conditions, can be recorded.

Since these individual events are beyond direct observation and the underlying dynamic process can only be inferred, every effort is being made to make these dynamic events reveal their occurrence by methods that are new and different from the former procedures.

Thus, to study the emission and absorption of quanta of energy and the collision of electrical particles, the investigator uses the Wilson Cloud Chamber which records the path of a single charge or particle as it passes through a vapor, or a Geiger counter which registers a single quantum emission. A variety of procedures are being used to elicit or record data on individual events by observing how they alter or disturb or leave a trace in a specially constructed situation or instrument sensitive to the specific events un-

----

[1] *Science*, 1943. 97 .. 1-7 .. 1943.

[2] *Note*: About 1900 young physicists could find no problem except the ever more precise measurement of the pressure, temperature and other characteristics of a gas.

der study, such as a fluorescent screen or photographic emulsion.

Another significant development has been the field concept which was described by Einstein and Infeld in *The Evolution of Physics*. They remark that

> It needed great scientific imagination to realize that it is not the charges nor the particles, but *the field in the space between charges and the particles*, which is essential for the description of physical phenomena. ... The theory of relativity arises from the field problems. The contradictions and inconsistencies of the old theories force us to ascribe new properties to the time-space continuum, to the scene of all events in our physical world. (p. 259)

Thus, instead of searching for a specific force or power believed to be resident in each particle or object or imputing a specific cause for each event, attention is being focussed upon the field in which events occur and the interrelations among particles and events which thereby create that field. Thus, physics is giving up the kind of *ad hoc* thinking so prevalent in psychology, of imputing specific motives or traits to individuals to account for their behavior or relying upon the conception of action at a distance. The newer formulations indicate that all behavior takes place in a field and can be understood as a function of that field, as we are now beginning to realize in the conception of the *cultural field* and the *social field* wherein patterned human conduct occurs. Physics explores and defines the field by a test body, the behavior of which reveals the organization of the field and its state and dynamic charges. The patterned conduct of the human organism reveals the operation of the cultural and social fields in which the individual has been reared and lives.

The field concept indicates that the older conception of "parts" and "wholes" and of "organization" will increasingly be modified. It seems clear that what we call "parts" are not the separate, discrete entities of our traditional analytic theory. Each "part" is an aspect or dimension of a complex of many dimensions which we have selectively observed and measured and named.

The "whole" is not "made up of parts," as we have been accustomed to think, conceiving the whole as another super-entity which is produced by parts, additatively. What we call "parts," by their interaction with other "parts" create and maintain that "whole" which, as a field, is constituted by the activities of the "parts." Thus, it would appear that the "parts" act, react and interact to create and maintain the "whole," as a field which simultaneously patterns the activities of the "parts," thereby giving rise to what we call "organization" which is not an entity but is this dynamic process. This is the conception emerging from atomic physics where the electrons are not viewed as entities but as states or activities which maintain the atomic organization of energy.

Thus, the field concept offers a promising lead to many older problems which can now be reformulated in these dynamic terms which introduce a number of new and fruitful ideas for research. The study of man and his varied activities, long pursued in terms of separate discrete organic "parts" and separate traits exhibited in isolated activities, can now be approached in these new terms with a resulting simplification and unification. The "organism as a whole," "holism" and similar concepts indicate how this new conception is being used, just as the conception of the personality reflects a similar recognition of the organization and interrelation of all the individual's functions and activities.

It is profoundly significant for scientific research, especially in the life sciences, to recognize that deviations around an established norm or central tendency are important for the study of convergent events where a multiplicity of anonymous units are interacting, giving rise to the relations between two dimensions or variables (e.g., pressure and temperature). But in the study of identified organisms, the crucial problem is the pattern or configuration in which the many dimensions of the organism appear. Here the focus is *not* upon deviations of one or two dimensions but upon the deformation or distortions of the generalized organic-personality pattern exhibited by the unique individual. These distortions may be structural (spatial) or functional (temporal) or energetical (the physical-chemical work performed or products produced), but they are revealed by the observation or, wherever possible, measurement of the whole organic complex to reveal the pattern or configuration. The persistence of the identifiable organism-personality while undergoing these distortions, deformations and disturbances involved in functioning and behaving, is now being recognized as a crucial problem.

It is no longer necessary nor valid to fractionate the organism-personality or reify our observations or measurements when we recognize them as dimensions of a multi-dimensional organization.

It becomes evident, when we think in terms of the field concept that every complex, physical, chemical, biological and social, is multi-dimensional. That is, each complex has many dimensions and offers a variety of data although not all the dimensions may be subject to measurement. We may observe a dimension but not be able to determine its magnitude. Each dimension is interrelated with the others, within the field of their patterned occurrence, where they have a *relative* magnitude, being functions of the "whole" of which each is a "part." Every measurement we make of any dimension must, therefore, be ordered to the field of its occurrence and given a relative magnitude and a location.

This is what the writer has called biological relativity to indicate the coming reformulation of concepts, problems and methodologies in the life sciences.[3]

This was clearly foreseen as long ago as 1885 when the elder Haldane prophetically said:

The problem of physiology is not to obtain piecemeal physico-explorations of physiological processes (I quote from the 1885 address),[4] but to discover by observation and experiment the *relatedness to one another of all the details of structure and activity in each organism* as expressions of its nature as *one* organism. . . . That a meeting place between biology and physical science may at some time be found there is no reason for doubting. But we may confidently predict that if that meeting point is found, and one of the two sciences is swallowed up, that one will not be biology.

The acceptance of the field concept and the multi-dimensionality of all complexes renders questionable the long established prac-

[3] Cf. the writer's papers, "Structure, Function and Growth," *Phil. of Science,* 2:2:210-235, April, 1935 and "Research in Orthopsychiatry," *Am. J. Orthopsychiat.,* XIII: 2-244-248, April, 1943.

[4] Sir Frederick Gowland Hopkins, "Some Chemical Aspects of Life," *Science,* 78: No. 2020, p. 227, September, 1933.

tices of reifying data into entities and treating dimensions and measurements as existents. We can fractionate wholes into "parts" only conceptually and after doing so we must reconstruct "whole" to understand the "parts."

How important this step may be for scientific research is indicated by the advances made in physics when they ceased reifying data. Thus, early in the Nineteenth Century investigators had made observations and gathered a variety of data on physical and chemical events. They had data on temperature, on light, electricity and magnetism, on mass and gravitation, and other physical and chemical events. But each of these data was reified into an entity, interpreted as indicating the presence of some special substance; for example, temperature data indicated the presence of a substance, heat; electrical data of a fluid, electricity, and so on. Each of these fictitious entities then gave rise to a special problem which later was "solved" by showing that these problems were generated by these fictitious entities, reified from data.

The great advance in physical thinking and the theoretical unification it has achieved came with the realization that these various data were not entities, but different dimensions of energy transformation propagated or transmitted through different media and appearing in different magnitudes which could be recorded and measured by appropriate instruments.

This has far reaching significance for the life sciences where we are accustomed to measure selected dimensions of structures, functions and activities, abstract these data from the complex or field of their occurrence and treat them as entities or existents, each of which must be "explained" in terms of the relation between two variables (dimensions) apart from the organic complex in which these dimensions occur, where each measurement has a relative magnitude. The familiar formulation of problems in terms of the relation between two variables, capable of being studied only by statistical methods, has a limited applicability in the study of organisms and their activities.

The experimental problem of establishing the meaning or significance of a datum is a problem of the relation between two variables, the datum and the space-time-energy event it reveals. But once the datum has been experimentally established, it can be fruitfully utilized only when it is associated with other data from the same energy complex to reveal the multi-dimensionality of that complex and the space-time events of its living activities. (Post mortem anatomical studies are artifacts.)

The problems in biology and psychology are rarely questions of the relation between two variables, abstracted from a complex but more often problems involving many dimensions since every structural form, functional process or activity arises from and expresses the organic whole and can be adequately studied only through a number of data. Indeed, the actual measurement of any organic dimension is significant primarily as relative to the other dimensions of that organism. As Dr. Holmes remarked many years ago, the relation of the size of a heart to the lungs *of an individual*, is more meaningful for understanding that individual organism, than the relation of that heart to other hearts from a thousand other individuals. It is the magnitude of any organ or functional activity in relation to other dimensions which is important for understanding an individual organism, as clinical medicine has shown.

Biological relativity recognizes the *relative* dimension of all measurements in biology and psychology and orders all measurements to the organic field in which they occur. It is obvious, for example, that each organ system of every individual differs in size but that size is relative to other organ systems in the same individual and to the whole organism. Moreover, any measurement, such as a millimeter, has a different relative significance in every part of an organism.

It is also significant that the purely quantitative problem of *how much* is being replaced by a search for discovering not only how much is present but how it is spatially arranged or located within the complex being studied. Thus, chemistry today has gone on, from the now simple quantitative determinations of two decades ago, to reveal the configuration of atoms within the molecules where the spatial arrangement of atoms is of major significance, as revealed by stereochemistry. Thus, the same atom in the same quantity, it is now known, produces different substances, depending upon its spatial location and attachment, as in stereoisomerism of the different sugars which rotate light to the right or left. The difference between an estrogen and a carcinogen, as in many other organic compounds, arises from the different spatial arrangement or attachment of the same atoms within the two spatially different molecules.

More and more of scientific research is being focussed upon the problem of patterns or configurations. Thus, in genetics it is being shown that it is not the number of genes but the specific location of the individual gene in the chromosome that gives a clue to its operation in organic development.

Schroedinger has recently suggested that the potentialities of the gene may be understood in terms of aperiodic solids which, like divergent events of quantum physics, initiate a series of non-repetitive events. (pp. 60-61)[5] Here the configural organization of atoms is of critical importance, as contrasted with numerical frequency or size.

Likewise, organic chemistry has shown that there are a number of basic patterns or configurations, as in proteins, wherein various additions and arrangements of supplementary atoms to this basic pattern give rise to the great variety of different proteins found in plants and animals.

To a large extent the amazing achievements in production of synthetics has become possible by the recognition of the spatial configurations of molecules and the possibility of detaching, substituting and rearranging and adding to the molecular pattern, something not conceivable in the older, purely quantitative conception of chemical compounds.

These developments have a large significance for the life sciences since they indicate that the intensive development of purely quantitative methods and large scale statistical studies, no matter how precise, can yield only limited understanding of some of these basic problems, involving dynamic processes, configural patterns and field relations, as exhibited by the individual organism-personality.

With these changing conceptions, there has been a growing concern for the study of the dynamics of events and the *process*

---

[5] *What is Life*, Macmillan, New York, 1945.

which produces the products we have learned to measure so carefully.[6] It is now recognized that the same basic or underlying *process* may produce different *products*, when operating under varying conditions, in different fields or upon different constituents. Conversely, it appears that different *processes* may produce similar or equivalent *products* under appropriate conditions.

Thus, the same basic processes of digestion, assimilation and metabolism operate in many diverse organisms, each of which selectively absorbs and utilizes the common foodstuffs of amino-acids, carbohydrates, fats, minerals and vitamins, to produce and maintain its characteristic organic structure and functions. As the familiar observation has pointed out, sheep eat corn and produce wool; pigs eat corn and produce hair and hides. This is accounted for by their different heredity but these genetic differences are operating through the generalized processes of nutrition, shared by both species, whereby each converts the same nutrients into different products.

That different processes may produce much the same *products* has been shown by the discovery of so many surrogates for the supposedly necessary, indispensable "causes." Thus, the eggs of various marine species have been artificially fertilized and similar substitutions have been performed on other organisms. The amazing development of synthetics has been made possible by chemical processes (sometimes simpler and sometimes more complicated) which man can manipulate to produce equivalents of naturally occurring products or to produce new products.

It is significant that scientific thinking and investigations are focussed today upon the study of process, superseding to a large extent the earlier preoccupation with precise measurement of spatial and temporal dimensions of the tangible, visible, easily manipulated forms and structures and the accessible end products of various processes.

There are recurrent, almost uniform, processes and also stable patterns and configurations giving rise to repeated products. These can be observed and measured to reveal the statistical regularities

[6] Cf. the writer's paper, "Gerontology," *Gerontology*, Vol. I, No. 1, p. 1-12, 1946.

and larger uniformities where the deviations are subordinated to the determination of central tendencies. Or these same processes and patterns can be studied to reveal the dynamic operation of the process and the occurrence of the discrete, discontinuous event which is variable and often unpredictable.

Scientific research, therefore, recognizes two large classes or divisions of problems: one, the search for regularities in large aggregates of more or less disorderly events with deviations to be revealed by statistical studies of convergent events and by the recurrent patterns and configuration that are more or less stable; two, the study of process, especially as exhibited in the divergent event and in the unique individual configuration or complex, such as the organism-personality.

This dual character of all events is found in the sub-atomic, atomic and molecular, molar and in larger configurations, such as organisms or constellations. It also appears in the recurrent regularities of conduct exhibited by members of a cultural group and a social order where each conforms to and deviates from the established patterns and practices of his society and traditions but in his or her individualized way.

Today, as in physics a few years ago, psychologists are divided between the classical group who insist that only statistical regularities and the relation between two variables are scientific, and others who are intent upon exploring dynamic processes and studying the uniquely individual. This split will be resolved, as it has been resolved in physics, when it is realized that the two problems are both legitimate, each approachable by different procedures and in terms of different conceptual formulations.

Scientific imagination is required to discover the similarity or equivalence of *process* producing different products when operating in different complexes or individuals who differ markedly in all their quantitatively observed dimensions and products. Likewise, scientific imagination is needed to recognize the equivalent products arising from different processes, which equivalence is usually overlooked or rejected because the investigator is intent upon observing and measuring identical complexes or similar magnitudes, in order to establish statistical regularities and central tendencies or the relation between two variables (i.e., selected dimensions of the multi-dimensional complex under study).

It is especially difficult to devise methods which will permit study of a process with the minimum of interference with the dynamics of that process. Biology and psychology are limited by the principle of indetermination which, as in physics, asserts we cannot measure that which our instrument or procedure disturbs or distorts. It is much simpler to observe and measure the products of a process since they are more stable and accessible (than the dynamic process which produced them) and less subject to disturbance or distortion (cf. the cadaver or skeleton or tissue slice with the living organism or cells). Again, as in physics, it is necessary to recognize the observer as participating in the process being studied.

Within the past fifty odd years there has been a progressive development of methods and instruments for discovering the internal spatial organization, dimensions and arrangements of intact living organisms. Also methods have been developed for revealing the operations and functioning activities of organ systems otherwise inaccessible to observation. Likewise, methods have been devised for revealing the molecular and atomic structure and the patterns in which energy transformation occur. These methods make possible the study of dynamics and processes which heretofore eluded observation and recording.

As pointed out earlier, much ingenuity has been expended upon instruments, which like the Wilson Cloud Chamber, permit recording of discrete events and the study of the individual units.

Newer Scientific Methods and Procedure

The internal structure and organization and the operations of any substance or organism can now be examined by various instruments and techniques with minimal interference or disturbance. X-rays provided the first such approach, permitting the investigator to "see" within any opaque complex organization and reveal its internal structural organization and dimensions. With refinements and elaborations and the use of special fluids almost all of the organ systems can now be photographed or observed as they function on the fluorescent screen. Stereoscopic x-rays now provide a means for precisely locating any point within the organism. X-rays have also been used for investigating the internal structure and organization of various substances, such as metals, rocks and also organic substances such as fibres; the x-rays in passing through are scattered or diffracted in characteristic patterns by the internal physical-chemical structure or organization of each substance. These diffraction patterns, like fingerprints, are now the accepted method of discovering the molecular and atomic patterns that give rise to the characteristic behavior of different substances. This has made possible the development of stereochemistry and new methods in biology, which will be described later.

The most recent instrument for investigating the finer structure of substances is the electron microscope which passes a stream of electrons through the substance under study and focusses them magnetically as they issue upon a screen. Here again amazing advances have been made by this method which, like x-rays, makes the complex being studied reveal its internal organization and fine structure beyond the range of usual optical instruments by the pattern it imposes upon the stream of electrons passing through. The internal structure and the intermolecular and interatomic activities and relations can then be validly inferred from these patterns.

By bombarding the atoms with electrical particles and recording the consequent alterations in their direction and energy, it has been possible to discover the atomic organization of elements and more recently, with slower particles, to release some of the organized energy within the atom with an accompanying transmutation of elements. This release of energy occurs with the dis-organization of the atom and its immediate reorganization of the charges that remain in the atomic field. As in the organism, a functional process takes place by a deformation of structure.

Spectrographic analysis is another method for revealing the chemical composition of any unknown substance. Each substance under appropriate conditions will emit light which can be distributed by a ruled grating along a spectrum. The coarse and fine lines in this spectrum not only identify each chemical substance but increasingly can be used to measure the amounts present in the sample under scrutiny. Thus spectrographic analysis has made it possible for astronomy to discover the chemical constituents of the sun and other stars by the characteristic lines of each element and its different states and experimentally to validate such interpretations.

The fluorescent microscope provides another method of revealing the composition of a substance by the way it fluoresces under ultraviolet light.

These methods are indicative of the newer procedures which have been devised to make a complex reveal its internal organization, composition, dynamic organization or state by the way that complex emits or absorbs radiations, patterns and responds to various forms of energy or behaves under different conditions in different fields.

If the complex or substance can be made to give off radiations, the mass spectrograph can determine its composition by the rate of travel of the particles it emits in a magnetic field. If the substance is exposed to various kinds of energy, heat, light, electricity, its composition can be discovered by the way it responds to that exposure or patterns that energy.

Light has been especially fruitful of newer methodologies and instruments. Polarized light passed through a substance will reveal its composition and molecular orientation by the way it interferes with or rotates that light. Light reflected by a monomolecular film of a substance also indicates the composition of that substance. Then, also, there are innumerable color indicators in chemical investigations, as well as electrical indicators, which reveal the state or composition of a substance by their electrical discharge or by their response to a current (pH determinations).

One of the highly significant developments in recent scientific research has been the establishment of indicators by which it is possible to discover the presence of a substance in an unknown or of a state or condition in an organism. These indicators have been set up by a procedure which is highly relevant to the question of reliability and validity.

Most of these indicators have been provided by starting with a known substance or state, accepted as such by all investigators. The way this known, identified substance or state reacts to a reagent, or colors a solution, or bends and distorts light or conducts a current is then experimentally determined, as attributable only to that substance or state, and so far as possible is quantitatively measured. This same procedure is then applied to any unknown, where the presence of the identified substance or state is revealed by this experimentally established reaction, color, etc.

It will be observed that the procedure starts with a known and establishes its characteristic signal or datum which then can be interpreted whenever it occurs in an unknown substance or condition. The validity of these tests is established, not by a statistical manipulation of a series of unknowns, but by showing the unequivocal relation of the datum to the identified substance or state it signifies. Moreover, reliability of the indicator is determined by the same procedure of working from a known substance and establishing the dependability of the indicator for that known substance to a carefully established degree of precision, by repeated experimental trials.

The individual components of a substance or of an organic compound may be discovered by electrophoresis which permits the separation, without injury or alteration, of different kinds of cells and colloids, as they move through a magnetic field and separate into components with definite boundaries.

Metallic ores and coal can be analyzed, i.e., made to reveal their composition and ash content, by the "angle of wetability," the angle of reflection or the color of light when reflected from a liquid film adhering to the surface of the unknown substance. Thus, the coal or ore can be analyzed without disintegration and fractional analysis.

In biological assays the responses of a living organism, its growth, development, reproductive capacity, longevity, etc., as in a mold or plant or animal, are used as indicators, if not measurements, of the potency of vitamins, hormones, virus, drugs, and other substances or living conditions.

Much of modern medicine has been made possible by various tests which enable the physician to discover the functional efficiency and pathology of organ systems and physiological processes by the individual patient's performance under certain loads or with specially devised substances that can be located or identified within the organism or found more or less modified in its excretions. Indeed, these medical tests and examinations are predicated upon the well established assumption that each patient functions in the basic patterns of mammalian physiology, which, however, operate uniquely in the individual according to his age, sex, state, condition, infections, etc., including his persistent affective reactions of anxiety and hostility. Medicine, it should be remembered, has long recognized the individual's *variability*, that is, his continually changing dimensions, as contrasted with *variation*, that is, differences among individuals. Medicine has had to look for syndromes, or patterns, within which individual variability could be interpreted relatively.

These newer methodological procedures and instruments are being refined and extended because they are essential for research as now directed by new concepts which go beyond the older static idea of a fixed structure or form and the older belief in a separate activity called function. Today it is becoming clear that we can measure *spatially* (structure or morphology), and *temporally* (function), quantifying the energy transformations involved, but we cannot rigidly separate these dimensions. These new concepts and methods offer possibilities for ascertaining what is either undiscoverable by other names, or is undeterminable by the analytic methods which interfere, fractionate, or destroy what is to be studied.

These newer procedures are more congruous with the newer conceptions of scientific study and permit the study of organized wholes and of organization, especially configurations and patterns and fields, approached as a dynamic process. Moreover, many of these newer methods permit the study of the specific, identified individual part, event or organism which heretofore was ignored or lost in the mass observations or obscured in the statistical compilations of two variables observed in anonymous, non-identified individuals or parts.

It should be recognized that *the concept of individuality has been extended by the discovery of how frequently the unique individual exists in nature*. Thus, it is apparent that each organism is different in most of its dimensions, more especially the configuration or pattern in which those dimensions occur. Thus, there is an individuality of functional operations and of chemical composition, as shown by experiments in transplantation of organs and glands between members of the same species.[7]

It is also recognized that *the proteins of different species and of each individual organism may be more or less unique in that the basic protein molecule is capable of almost indefinite variation by the incorporation of different substances which change the individual's protein.*

Immunology also has shown the unique individual organism who develops specific immunities and antigens, susceptibilities, allergies and similar reactions. The process called anaphalaxis wherein an organism may become sensitized by one injection of a foreign protein so that it will die of shock upon a second injection, is highly individualized (like the traumatic experiences of an individual personality).

The foregoing abbreviated discussion of recent scientific developments may serve to indicate how psychology, and also psychiatry and psychoanalysis, are being impeded by reliance upon earlier concepts and methods which are no longer appropriate to the new problems now emerging in the field of personality study and diagnosis. It seems probable that as the younger students and practitioners in these fields become more aware of, and familiar with, this emerging new climate of opinion, they will vigorously move on to a systematic reformulation of now accepted concepts and theories and the further development and refinement of these promising methods and procedures.

[7] See Leo Loeb, *The Biological Basis of Individuality*, Thomas, 1945.

III

APPROACHES TO THE STUDY OF PERSONALITY

THE approaches to study of personality have, of necessity, been directed by the conceptions and assumptions and the methodologies of each discipline.

Psychiatrists have developed their concepts, largely shaped within the past few decades by psychoanalytic assumptions and methods which emphasize the dynamic aspects of personality and the genesis of conduct and feelings in early experience. In accordance with the medical tradition, the psychiatrists rely upon the patient's history for their basic data which they attempt to validate, sometimes by a case history obtained by a social worker or by prolonged, intensive testing of the patient's own testimony and interpretation of whatever he says or does in terms of their basic theoretical assumptions.

As the lawyers have long recognized, testimony is probably the most unreliable of all evidence and without corroboration cannot be accepted as valid, reliable data. But the psychiatrist operates with the further assumption that testimony, however factually false and misleading, may nevertheless be utilized to understand the dynamic process of personality formation and operation by its symbolic representation of what life experience has meant to the patient and how he has felt about it. Psychologists have used testimony in questionnaires and self-rating sheets, often without corroboration or interpretation.

The clinical interpretation of testimony and of life history records has provoked criticism and rejection by those who cannot accept what seems to be a wholly arbitrary process of symbolic interpretation of behavior which the psychiatrist either cannot or will not submit to their criteria of credibility or their procedures for testing reliability and validity.

In these controversies one may see the operation of somewhat disparate, if not conflicting, assumptions and criteria, one derived from an earlier climate of opinion and older frame of reference, the other emerging from the newer climate of opinion and newer criteria of credibility. Thus, to the classical physicist the early findings and theoretical interpretations of quantum physics were often unacceptable because the classical assumptions and methods demanded statistical evidence as contrasted, for example, with the evidence of a Wilson Cloud Chamber (recording the path of a single charge) or some other procedure used in quantum or atomic physics.

It must be recognized that data are only data which have little objective significance. They become meaningful and credible only in the context of a conceptual scheme with assumptions that are tested, not so much by the data, as by the internal consistency and congruity of the concepts and assumptions of the investigators using these data and the kind of logic they utilize. This is the lesson derived from mathematics which has repeatedly developed new types of order, wholly at variance with the prevailing interpretation of data and the accepted logical concepts and expectations, only to be accepted later and utilized to order observations and to build a new conceptual formulation more adequate for ordering data then obtained by new procedures.

Psychiatry still faces the task of conceptual clarification and the resolution of many internally inconsistent theoretical elements. It also is vulnerable to the criticism of violating the principle of parsimony in creating so many *ad hoc* mechanisms and psychic entities for its theoretical formulations (such as the id, ego and superego). But in the practice of interpreting data according to a conceptual scheme and imputing dynamic processes to human behavior, the psychiatrist cannot be fairly or successfully challenged by the frequent demand for "objective" evidence.

Psychologists, with some exceptions, have approached the problem of personality, directed by the prevailing assumptions and conceptual formulations of their discipline, or the sub groups in the psychological profession. Perhaps the largest group has been the psychometrists who have applied the techniques of standardized test construction to personality tests or factor analysis to reveal traits or clusters of traits. They have conceived of personality as another kind of individual difference, to be measured or rated by a test which was statistically reliable and valid for an adequate sample of population of a given age, sex, etc.

In this approach they have been guided by the evident regularities of human behavior since each member of a society must utilize the socially approved patterns of action, speech, belief and feelings which can be statistically established as the central tendencies among the individual deviations from these norms. For each age, sex and other identifiable group, the appropriate norms can be established and then utilized in various tests to discover where the individual stands in relation to these group norms. The individual can then be rated in terms of his conformity to, or deviation from, these norms and further classified by various categories or diagnostic grouping assigned to those deviations.

It is obvious that such tests and the various inventories also used to discover where the individual stands in relation to a group, give valuable and significant findings about the individual in terms of *group norms.* The reliability and validity of such tests are indicative of the *group,* not of the *individual* being tested or rated because the statistical procedures employed of necessity ignore the identifiable individual as a unique personality, treating him as one of many similar anonymous units, differing only in deviations from the group norms.

As pointed out earlier, this procedure is the method of classical physics which was concerned with the order and regularity of mass events, like thermodynamics and gas laws where enormous members of particles or molecules converged into certain statistically frequent patterns. These methods assumed that the individual particle or molecule was insignificant and could be ignored since the important factor was the recurrent, persistent regularities arising from the host of anonymous units.

It was not until quantum physics brought a realization of individual quanta and a concern for identifiable events that these statistical methods were supplemented by the newer methods and procedures briefly described earlier. There is no conflict between the classical and quantum physics today because it is recognized that they are concerned with two aspects of events, the convergent and divergent, to use Langmuir's terms, or the anonymous or identifiable, and they use either statistical methods or probability or the procedures described earlier (Cloud Chamber, diffraction patterns, etc.).

The psychological procedures which utilize the subject's response to standardized questions on a test, inventory or questionnaire rely upon the subject's testimony or even self-diagnosis, as expressed in words. The historical development of our language has loaded many words, especially those concerned with people and human behavior, with many animistic and dualistic implications. These, we are now realizing, often obscure the very process that the methods are designed to reveal. It is relevant to point out that the elaborate systems of traits which have been constructed are essentially collections of words taken from the dictionary, sorted into categories of similar meaning or even synonyms. These words likewise are loaded with an amazing variety of animistic implications, often alien to the contemporary scientific approach. When, as some studies have done, these words from a dictionary are treated as *data* on personality, we have the extraordinary situation of scientific research using words as if they were data of observation, indeed, reifying such words into entities to be handled by factor analysis, offered as seemingly empirical findings on living personalities.

What is important here is that *the same words and phrases may be understood and used by different individuals with widely different meaning.* Moreover, different words and phrases may be understood or used by different individuals with the same meanings, so that subjects and patients as well as scientific investigators of personality may be involved in an impossible confusion of words.

It is also obvious that individuals are under social pressure and often are compelled by their own personal experience to conceal what they actually think or believe or feel. Hence, the individual is likely to fit himself into the categories and to utilize the words which he believes to be socially acceptable, suppressing others. This aspect of an individual's responses or beliefs is recognized by the psychiatrist who is clinically trained to look beyond the patient's words to their probable meaning and emotional significance.[1] In a standardized test this rarely occurs because the test results usually can be interpreted only in the terms of the standardized meanings and categories of the test construction with no further access to the subject tested.

Some personality inventories are designed to elicit additional responses to the same questions or similar topics in different contexts in order to test the credibility of the subject's responses by the internal congruity or incongruity of his aggregate responses. But these inventories usually aim at a diagnostic classification of the patient about whom as a personality little is revealed unless the inventory items are interpreted as indicators of the individual personality.

This is the dilemma of the standardized procedure, that in order to use only "objective" data (not now referring to the trait collections), it must be content with group norms and ignore the question of reliability and validity *for any single, identifiable individual personality*. Thus, the standardized procedure cannot be expected to give much light upon individual personality, as unique individuals. Nor can they contribute much insight into the dynamic processes of personality. In saying this, one does not attack or reject standardized tests but rather indicates what they can and cannot do.

The clinically trained psychologists who have become expert in administering and scoring standardized mental and performance tests usually develop the clinical ability to interpret these tests for understanding personality over and above the quantitative ratings (as in item analysis). Many clinical psychologists are primarily concerned with diagnoses and treatment of personalities and they operate with more or less eclectic conceptions and methods. It is interesting to note that some psychologists who prefer statistical methods and factor analyses prefer to work on test data without ever seeing or interviewing subjects or patients, as if they were interested not in personalities but in mathematical-statistical operations upon quantitated data.

---

[1] It has been shown that the patient's language can be studied as a patterning of verbalizations, wholly apart from content or meaning, since each individual uses words in a pattern which is clinically significant of personality makeup and disturbances. (Eliot Chapple)

The long established concepts, methods and criteria of credibility in psychology, like those in classical physics, are in process of being supplemented and extended, to recognize the newer concepts, the different methods and more recently developed criteria, as they have in quantum physics and the dynamic interpretation of events.

Here is where the psychocultural approach offers a promising lead. It conceives of the individual personality as a dynamic process whereby the individual creates, maintains and defends his "private world." This private world arises from the individual's taking over and utilizing all the patterns of our cultural traditions, but doing so in his own peculiar idiomatic way, with the feelings that his experiences in childhood have established as his susceptibilities and his immunities and persistent affective reactions.

There are recurrent regularities of human conduct, as pointed out earlier, since each individual must utilize the socially sanctioned norms of action, speech, belief and feelings, and carry on his life activities in the social prescribed practices of contract, barter, sale, employment, courtship and marriage, voting, litigation, and the like. To be understood and accepted, the individual must act, react and interact with others in these common patterns and practices. By this patterned participation, he, with all others, creates the social order, or what we call social organization, as earlier defined. Moreover, the aggregate of these patterned activities of many individuals gives rise to what we call social, economic and political "forces," which are not large scale forces acting at a distance, but rather are the aggregate of many individual patterned acts, just as the pressure and other statistical regularities of the gas is the product of innumerable individual molecules, interacting to produce such statistical regularities.

Here it is appropriate to point out that any kind of test can be utilized as a projective method if the subject's performance or responses are treated, not as products to be rated, but as indicators to be interpreted. Thus, item analyses, the individual's choice of words or responses or combination of responses, considered apart from group norms, may be considered as an individual personality production to the test, as in any other projective method.

The current controversy in psychology over projective methods seems to be similar to that which for a number of years raged in physics when the newer concepts and methods of quantum physics were rejected by those who preferred the classical theories and procedures of the older physics. It will be recalled that for a while, as one physicist said, "Physics was classical on Monday, Wednesday and Friday, and quantum on Tuesday, Thursday and Saturday." This difference has largely been resolved, as indicated in the earlier quotation from Langmuir, by the realization that physical events may be approached in two ways, the search for convergent large scale regularities and the search for divergent, quantum events.

The resolution of the present conflicts in psychology, over personality studies, like the conflict over atomistic sensation or gestalt, will come with a clearer realization of these two aspects of events, these two kinds of scientific interests which are both legitimate and scientifically valid.

It is disturbing, however, to see how some of the statistically inclined students seem to be determined to prevent any non-statistical study of personality to be recognized or carried on in their universities. It was also disturbing to see during the war how the statistically trained psychologists seemed to be so resistant to the recognition of the clinically trained psychologist in the war program of selecting personnel and especially of screening out personalities.

This professional rivalry and reluctance to accept any new development which diverges from the long established patterns are understandable in psychology, as they were in physics. They are deplorable, however, when they impede the free use of intelligence and block the interest and curiosity of younger students who should be inducted into the science of today, not the science of their teacher's youthful student days.

In view of the enormous problems ahead when we must provide for the understanding of personality development and expression in schools and industry, as well as the armed forces, and must screen large numbers, it is evident that this present professional situation cannot long continue.

Thus, in discussing projective methods, it must again be stated that they are not offered as a rival or competitor to standardized tests and inventories or other "non-projective" methods.[2] The use of projective methods for further investigation of personality development and expression and for clinical diagnoses and treatment (including evaluation of treatment) seems essential if psychology is to go on as an advancing scientific discipline, prepared to make its contribution not only to the advancement of knowledge but to the exigent social and personal problems pressing for attention.

Nuclear fission became possible only when physics developed the new concepts and methods of atomic physics as contrasted with classical physics. Field theory, as indicated by the earlier quotation from Einstein and Infeld, became possible when attention was transferred from a search for inner forces and action at a distance to a concern with the space-time field in which events take place.

A somewhat similar situation is occurring in psychology. For generations we have tried to understand human conduct and personality expression as the outward and visible evidence of specific traits, motives, *ad hoc* forces and other conceptions of a *vis a tergo* or a Maxwell demon-soul, guiding the individual like the pilot of a ship. The theory and the methods were all in terms of something inside the individual, while the social-cultural world in which he lived and conducted his affairs was considered an objective world offering only objective stimuli or bodily satisfactions (like food), or passive situations to be manipulated.

Today in the conception of a private world which the individual himself creates and maintains and so far as possible imposes upon the surrounding world of people, things and events (according to cultural patterns), we can make a step forward similar to relativity and space-time. Today we account for the path of a planet, star, or other body by ordering its motion to the curved space-time which provides the path of least travel and so derives the observed motion from the field of the observed action.

So we can account for the personality, its action, speech, beliefs and feelings, its ideas and its conduct, as a function of the warped,

[2] Cf. "Non-Projective Personality Tests," *Annals of N. Y. Academy of Science,* Vol. XLVI, Art. 7, pp. 531-678, 1946.

often distorted, private world of the individual personality who imposes that warping, that distortion, that selective organization, meaning and affective significance upon the social and cultural world which he, along with all other members of the group, maintains by his individual activity. Individual personalities, idiomatically using the prescribed social and cultural patterns, create the social and cultural space-time, just as the individual molecules in a gas create the gas, while each deviates from that norm or statistically most frequent pattern.

Thus, we can begin to order our observations upon human conduct and personality to the field of that personality's private world, thereby dispensing with most of the complicated mechanisms and more or less esoteric entities of psychiatric-psychoanalytic theory and psychological terminology. But we must retain their dynamic conception of personality and reinterpret the amazing insights developed by the clinical students of personality in this other frame of reference.

In passing, it may be remarked that this conception of the personality as emerging from a cultural field, as maintained and transmitted by parents and teachers, makes possible an epidemiological approach to personality disturbances and mental disorders in terms of the persistent traditional ideas, beliefs and practices which operate to warp and distort the private world of children and adolescents. By discovering these traditional patterns and establishing them as the source of the socially destructive and self-defeating personality private worlds, we can begin to disinfect and cleanse the cultural environment, as we have learned to free the geographical environment of infected water and milk and parasites and carriers of disease.

But as the reader must now be aware, *we must be prepared to give up much of the older, now anachronistic, if not archaic, assumptions and conceptions about personality if we are to proceed in this direction.*

Projective methods for the study of personality may then be viewed in the light of the foregoing and their purpose and significance understood as expressions of the new climate of opinion we are now entering.

IV

PROJECTIVE TECHNIQUES

WHEN the personality is conceived as a dynamic process, it can be approached through a study of its functioning and operations and its various products.

The recently developed scientific procedures described earlier offer leads to new methods of investigating the personality process as a dynamic operation, revealing the individual's unique way of organizing and interpreting experience and reacting with feelings of greater or less intensity thereto.

The problem presents these two aspects: (a) *the generalized process of personality development and operation,* and (b) *its idiomatic functioning in each specific individual who thereby develops and maintains his "private world," as a unique dynamic configuration.*

The personality process involves a selective awareness of all situations, as patterned by the prior experience of the individual who has been sensitized or rendered more or less anesthetic, so that he sees, hears and otherwise perceives what has become relevant and meaningful to him and ignores or rejects all else. The process operates also in the individual's peculiar personal way of fitting whatever he has selectively perceived into the more or less unique pattern, configuration, or organization of his private world, of interpreting and defending it and dealing with it, always according to its meaning and emotional significance for him.

It must be reiterated here that the generalized patterns derive from the cultural traditions of each group of people. Thus, there are certain regularities of action, speech, belief and feeling (the *eidos* and *ethos* of a culture) which will be utilized by all individuals, just as they use the common language in their attempts to communicate. These recurrent, statistically demonstrable modes of conduct are the norm around which individuals deviate.

But, as pointed out earlier, the same, almost identical actions and words may have diverse significance because each individual uses these actions and words with his or her own peculiar personal meaning, in a context of his or her own private world. Moreover, different individuals may exhibit different, almost contradictory, activities or speech which have the same or equivalent significance in the private worlds of each (as, for example, in the religious beliefs and prayers of different sects).

Data, as we have earlier seen, must not be reified into entities nor can the observed activities of individuals be interpreted as "forces" or "powers" or motives or traits or similar expressions of a *vis a tergo* or a Maxwellian demon operating these observed activities.

Like the organization and activities within the atom, we cannot directly observe but must infer these operations of the personality process from a variety of observations, clinical and experimental, showing the dynamic way in which the personality process acts upon all experience, patterning, warping, bending, distorting and otherwise converting every situation or experience into the configuration of the individual's private world, so far as it can be so manipulated. When not capable of being manipulated, the personality can ignore or "rationalize" it.

This process is not something subjective and "psychic," but is like all other dynamic processes through which events are organized and patterned into configurations and unique individualities. As indicated earlier, man with his large brain, his capacity for ideas and imagination and skilled hands for manipulation, has developed his cultural world as a way of transforming nature into a symbolic world, organized and interpreted according to the basic beliefs and assumptions of his traditions. The personality process operates in maintaining this symbolic cultural world and the prevailing social order, as all members of a group utilize similar patterns in all their thinking, believing, speaking and actions, thereby creating the cultural "field."

Thus, we may observe the generalized process and the more or less regular, recurrent patterns in this cultural field of the group life. But, since each individual personality has accepted, rejected and modified these generalized patterns and taken them over into his private world in unique configurations and with the peculiar meanings and emotional significances he imposes upon all situations, we may study the individual personality process, not primarily as exhibited in deviations from these social norms, but in the dynamic patterns and persistent processes that the individual utilizes when employing these norms and conventional practices as directed by his private world.

For example, to understand the personality process of an individual, it will not give much light to measure his use of the socially approved monetary practices—how much money he receives and uses, metallic and paper, in the customary practice of buying and selling, along with others. Nor will it give much illumination to discover the magnitude of his income and of his various expenditures, as such. But how he uses these pecuniary practices and symbols, outwardly like others or even illegally, but individually contrived and applied, for his own peculiar personality expression, may be of large significance in understanding his personality, along with his use of other socially approved practices and rituals.

An organic analogy may also be cited. The members of a given genus or species will exhibit the generalized organic structures and functions of their phylogenetic pattern, but each member of that species will deviate from these generalized patterns. This regularity and diversity is largely biological and so is limited in the range of non-lethal variations. But the human personality is a genotypical development within a cultural field which itself may be either uniform and stable, only slowly changing, or may be more or less confused, conflicting and changing at different rates for different patterns, as we see in western European culture today.

Here we must accept the principle of biological relativity and recognize that the objectively observed and recorded activity of the individual, measured whenever possible, becomes significant for understanding that individual only when interpreted in terms of its relative magnitude and its meaning or relationships within the "field" or the configuration of its occurrence, i.e., the private world of the personality. Thus, it has been shown that the same atom plays a different rôle in each compound according to its location in the molecular configuration. Likewise, the same magnitude has a different relative dimension in each organic configuration where it is one of many other dimensions of that organism, as shown by clinical medicine. Moreover, different magnitudes may be organized or related in similar patterns, like a triangle.

Every action and every spoken word of the individual becomes meaningful for understanding that individual when and as interpreted according to the significance which the individual himself gives them. This is not unlike the way each organism utilizes the same foodstuffs and the basic molecular patterns, as in proteins, to develop its specialized structures and functions and unique protein molecules. Nor is it different from the way in which organisms utilize different substances and situations for similar or almost identical activities, such as nest building or food storage, as they pattern and convert portions of the environment into the forms or the operations each requires for its specialized mode of existence.

Whenever an observation or measurement of an individual is abstracted from that individual, as in a frequency distribution, it loses its significance for understanding *that individual*, although it may be of value for study of other and more general problems, as now recognized in physics in convergent and divergent events.

One might say that the *single* or *dual* observations or measurements of an anonymous organism can be meaningful and significant only when they are treated as one of a large series of such observations, as in frequency distribution and the various statistical manipulations of mass data for correlations, factor analyses, etc.

Only when the single observation is combined with others, *from the same identifiable individual*, can it offer any significant clues to its meaning *for that individual*.

Thus, for the study of individuals as organisms and as personalities, it is necessary to make a number of observations and measurements on the same identified individual and to interpret those in terms of their meaning, significance and relative magnitudes for that identified individual.

Projective techniques are not new; they have been utilized in various ways for centuries but only recently have they been recognized and named as such and given a rationale congruous with our developing understanding of human conduct.[1]

It seems probable that much of the early, primitive jurisprudence employed projective techniques to judge the guilt or innocence of individuals. Trial by ordeal involved the exposure of the accused to stressful situations in which, as eating dry rice, he would respond in an individualized manner, indicative of his guilt, however he denied it or attempted to conceal his participation in the crime. Recently it has been suggested that the divination basket of the Bantu is a primitive projective method, the diviner interpreting the objects chosen from the basket by each individual.

Shakespeare repeatedly refers to what are essentially projective techniques. Thus, Hamlet tells Polonius to look at the animal forms in the clouds, thus presaging the Stern Cloud Pictures by three centuries. Again, when Hamlet instructs the players, he remarks that "The play's the thing, wherein I'll catch the conscience of the King," again foreshadowing the many uses of drama, as in puppet shows, play techniques and psychodrama and sociodrama, to evoke the reactions of the audience and to thereby discover their feelings of anxiety, guilt and hostility. Moreover, in Hamlet there is an explicit declaration of how each individual hears and interprets what is said, as in the speech

> . . . her speech is nothing,
> Yet the unshaped use of it doth move
> The hearers to collection; They aim at it
> And botch the words up, fit to their own
> thoughts . . . .

Basically, a projective technique is a method of studying the personality by confronting the subject with a situation to which he will respond according to what that situation means to him and how he feels when so responding. Thus, almost anything or experience can be utilized for projective techniques, including the standardized tests of intelligence, if the examiner will look for the idiomatic way (such as in item analysis) the subject has responded

[1] Cf. David Rappaport, *Diagnostic Psychological Testing*, Year Book Publishers, Chicago, 1945, Vol. 1, p. 10 and Vol. 2, p. 89.

to that test, as contrasted with the customary measurement of conformity to age or other norms. Classroom recitations and writings also offer similar materials for understanding individuals.

This point needs to be reëmphasized again and again. The standardized test uses the group norms to measure the individual's conformity to or deviation from the standard of conventional performance. The projective method is concerned with the idiomatic expression or response of the individual, as revealed in the context of his other expressions, activities and feelings.

The essential feature of a projective technique is that it evokes from the subject what is, in various ways, expressive of his private world and personality process. The projective technique gives the subject the opportunity to invest situations with his own meaning, to impose upon them his own values and significance, especially affective significance. What is important is that the situation be sufficiently plastic and unstructured to permit this imposing of these personal forms and meanings, or, if organized and structured, to allow the subject to manipulate or react to the situation or its constituents in his own individualized way. It is like driving a car; there must be streets or roads open for the driver to pilot his car and allow him to exhibit his personal style of driving.

Thus, projective techniques may range from wholly amorphous, plastic, ductile materials to the highly conventionalized situations, activities and symbols or patterns which each subject utilizes or responds to, in his own idiomatic fashion.

One way of classifying projective techniques is to see them as belonging to different patterns, depending upon what they require or seek to evoke from the subject. Thus, there are:

1. Constitutive methods which require the subject to impose some structure or organization upon the unstructured, plastic materials or only partially organized situation present to him.

2. Constructive methods which require the subject to arrange materials with definite size or shape or pattern into larger configurations, including the sorting of diverse objects.

3. Interpretive methods which elicit from the subject an interpretation of some experience or some composition in which he finds a personal meaning or affective significance.

4. Cathartic methods which not only reveal the personality process of the subject by what he finds therein but also permit and encourage his emotional or chronic affective reactions. (It is probable that every projective technique offers an occasion for some emotional or affective reaction; but some are specifically designed for that purpose.)

5. Refractive methods which give clues to the subject's personality process by the way he alters or distorts a conventional medium of communication, such as language or handwriting, as idiomatically used by each personality.

In all these methods the subject is required to do something which will reveal how he organizes experience, interprets situations and events, and feels toward life. Like the more recently developed methods in physical science, the purpose is to make the dynamic process disclose its operation, either directly or indirectly, in situations, materials or activities sufficiently plastic or labile to permit their manipulation or distortion for projective reactions.

CONSTITUTIVE METHODS

These methods use highly diversified materials and situations to elicit from the subject some organization or structuralizing of the more or less amorphous or ambiguous material or partly structural situation.

The most highly developed and oldest of these methods is the Rorschach Ink Blot Test or procedure which employs a series of ten cards, each of which presents an ink blot, i.e., a symmetrical figure or shape, with different shades of black on a white background, and with colors in some of the cards.

These cards have been widely used and intensely studied in Europe and in the United States, often in clinics where the subjects have been carefully examined by psychiatrists and psychoanalysts, with detailed case histories and other materials. They have also been utilized in making physical, especially neurological, diagnoses (such as brain tumors) and in making prognoses for shock and other therapies, where they have been subject to critical evaluation in the light of subsequent operations or autopsies and of the patient's condition after therapy.

Because the cards present shapes or figures which are relatively unstructured and are, therefore, susceptible of being perceived and interpreted in various ways, they compel the subject to "see" in them what he imposes on them. In other words, every response he makes to the card is constitutive, an active selective process, of giving form and meaning to what the card offers him to organize and interpret.

In the response to the Rorschach cards the dynamic process of the personality operates upon the card and thereby reveals a variety of different aspects of that personality dynamics. This is not the occasion to elaborate upon these but it is sufficient to point out that various categories of responses have been developed which, *when interpreted along with all other responses*, have been established as highly significant.

Thus, the subject's responses may be to the *whole* blot or to parts, even to small *details*. It may be a *human* or *animal* form, to *movement* and to *color* or *shading*. More subtle interpretative criteria recognize location, the symbolic content of responses, and so on.

Each of these interpretive or diagnostic categories and subcategories reveal different aspects of the multi-dimensional private world of the subject and must be interpreted in that larger context, along with all the other responses which give each response its *relative* meaning and value.

The affective reaction of the subject is of major significance since the ink blots, especially those with color, may provoke either a strongly emotional response, expressed either overtly in words or in refusal to give a response ("color shock").

It is characteristic of projective methods that they are provocative of emotional reactions or affective responses, such as feelings of anxiety, of guilt or resentful hostility. They also reveal such personality characteristics as submissiveness, dominance or dependence, constriction or outgoing feelings, generosity or possessiveness, free flowing affectivity or anesthesia and similarly described dimensions of the personality process for which magnitudes can rarely be given.

The examiner must be clinically trained and alert to these expressions, not only when administering the procedure, but in interpreting the subject's initial verbal responses and during the inquiry or graphic responses.

This seemingly "subjective" process of interpretation has provoked much controversy and sometimes scornful rejection of Rorschach findings by those who insist that data must be not only quantitative, but purely *"objective"* according to the established criteria of statistical reliability and validity. There can be no satisfactory answer to this demand since, as pointed out above, this reliability and validity can be established only for group norms derived from anonymous individuals, treated as interchangeable units, differing only in their deviations from these norms. In other words, the critics of the Rorschach appear to believe that their criteria of credibility must govern all personality studies and diagnostic findings.

Just as quantum physics had to go beyond classical physics and invent new techniques and develop more appropriate criteria of credibility for study of quantum operations and for relativity-field problems, so the students of personality have had to depart from psychometric practices, as will be discussed later.

The Rorschach procedure operates with ink blots, like the Stern Cloud patterns which require the subject to organize and invest them with form and meaning. Here, it has been pointed out, is shown the difference between sensation and perception since the subject perceives something by patterning the purely visual sensations. It requires specific focus or deliberate effort, as years of laboratory studies have shown, for an individual to attend to or observe *a sensation*, by ignoring or selectively rejecting the context and perceptual pattern in and through which he otherwise naïvely responds to visual experiences.

Other materials or sensory toys provide for a similar operation by the subject, who can shape, manipulate and otherwise impose his personality process or express his feelings upon clay or plasticene or mud pies, or finger paints or any other plastic, flexible, unstructured material, including cold cream or malleable situation. Simple, free drawings, like "doodlings," with pencil or crayon, provide similar opportunities for the subject to reveal his personality process.

Formal or spontaneous art productions of all kinds, such as easel painting, sculpture or carvings, also provide projective materials for understanding the individual personality.

The range and variety of constitutive methods is almost unlimited because any of the sensory or functional capacities of an individual can be utilized for a constitutive response and an interpretive response. The color organ for presenting a continuous visual field of changing colors, fluidly merging into each other and modulating from one hue to another, as in music, provides a sequence of sensory experiences, like listening to music, which individuals may structuralize or respond to with images and also emotionally, or with chronic feelings of anxiety, guilt or hostility.

Ambiguous sounds, not clearly or fully enunciated, may be presented to a subject who imposes upon them a meaningful pattern of words and phrases. The pattern, sequence and rate of a subject's language, *regardless of content*, also are significant of his personality process.

The possibilities of smell and taste have not been thoroughly explored but with the coming of apparatus for presenting such stimuli in controlled situations, they will offer rich possibilities. Touch or kinesthetic responses have been explored as in various procedures in neurology (e.g., the Romberg) and other postural reactions of a subject to spatial orientation when blindfolded, in the dark, etc. Drawing a figure when the hands are obscured by a screen, as in Mira's myokinetic test and similar procedures, involve both perceptual and orientating patterns of individuals, in a free field of overt movement.

It is important to note that, as in all instruments, *there is encountered in projective methods, especially the constitutive procedures, the conflict between sensitivity and precision.* Stern's Cloud Pictures may be more sensitive (because entirely plastic and unstructured) than the partially structured ink blots which are, therefore, more precise in recording the subject's responses. Even the trivial mistakes of daily conversation when one person "misunderstands" what another says, hearing one word which differs from that actually spoken, can be utilized as projective responses. Too often these cannot be interpreted correctly because of lack of a context but they are as much a part of the "psychopathology" of everyday life as are the verbal slips and blunders.

CONSTRUCTIVE METHODS

While the constitutive methods require the subject to structuralize and impose meaning upon wholly ambiguous, plastic materials, the constructive methods present to the subject already shaped, formed objects, with either a specific, definitely recognizable meaning, such as housekeeping or miniature life toys with more generalized functions, such as wooden blocks for building or colored units for making a mosaic.

The subject is given a collection of these materials to put in order or to play with, or, if older and more sophisticated, to set a scene for the stage or moving pictures, or to make a model of an actual life scene. In utilizing these materials, both the generalized and the specific, the subject must organize or arrange them in a spatial pattern, which to some extent is limited by the specific toy or miniature objects, for example, miniature kitchen or bathroom equipment. The blocks are less specific or defined or limited in use and so can be used by the subject to enclose a space, build walls, towers, make a house, etc.

Within this enclosed space (if he so builds) the subject arranges the miniature life toys in accordance with his image or understanding of the life situation he is portraying, or as he may feel about it or may wish it to be. This is one of the initial difficulties because, in these constructions, the subject may project a combination of these and thereby initially confuse the observer. It calls for clinical judgment to decide whether the child does not yet know where certain objects or equipment belong in a house or whether he puts them (e.g., toilet bowl in the living room-parlor) in a conspicuous and uncommon room position because of their meaning and affective significance for him at that time in his life. Likewise, it is a question whether the child builds a house with no doors through inadvertant omission or to represent a tight world closed against intrusion.

Constructive methods, as Erik H. Erikson has pointed out,[2] provide the child with a *microcosm* through and in which he can deal with the *macrocosm* of the adult world and can express what is happening to the *autocosm* of his own body-internal world. They also permit the subject to reveal his personal frame of reference and way of organizing experience and conceptualizing the world, even by simple sorting and categorizing of miniature life toys.

Drawings and paintings may be considered constitutive, when wholly free and spontaneous, or may be treated as constructive when the subject is asked to draw a person or to draw a man or woman or other defined object or animal. These productions are significant of the individual's image of the body and his feelings, including psychosomatic disorders. They also may be indicative of the adult subject's early, preschool orientation since most adults have not gone beyond the four or five year old level of drawing; hence, their drawings may reveal how they viewed the world and felt toward situations when they ceased to draw (as Cameron has shown).

Here it may be appropriate to point out that under hypnosis, or drugs, the individual may be released from the restrictions and demands of the contemporary social world. Accordingly, when given permission by the therapist, he may do and say what is revealing of his otherwise concealed private world and personality process, including early stages in his personality development. In doing so, the subject, like the child with miniature life toys, acts as if the actual world of things and people were again plastic and fluid, capable of approach and treatment according to his characteristic personality patterns, especially at an earlier stage of his life career.

It is important to recognize that *what a subject does in a projective situation may be directly constitutive or constructive, expressing or revealing more or less faithfully his private world and characteristic personality process.* Or his projective productions

2 "Configurations in Play," *Psychoanalyt. Quart.*, 1937, 6, pp. 139-214.

may be only symbolic of that private world and especially of the subject's affective reactions.

This symbolism may be interpreted in a detailed way, by giving to each object or figure a symbolic meaning or representative significance, such as treating a male doll figure as a representative of the subject's father, etc. Or the symbolic interpretation may be given to the pattern or configuration of the subject's arrangement, such as a house or room with no doors or windows, or furniture crowded or stacked together in a narrow room or the transposition of the bathroom-toilet equipment. Placing members of the family (e.g., father sleeping in garage) also may reveal the child's feelings toward his family. Or, again, any representation may be given a symbolic significance such as the interpretation of a boat as a mother symbol, etc.

The extent to which symbolic interpretations will be made depends largely upon the conceptual scheme of the clinician which may range from simple representation to elaborate disguises, as in earlier dream interpretation.

The important point to emphasize here is not the specific kind of interpretation but the underlying process of eliciting what the subject otherwise cannot or will not reveal about his way of organizing and maintaining and defending his private world.

In passing, it may be remarked that projective methods, especially the construction and interpretative methods, make it possible to obtain projective productions while the subject, especially the child, is engaged in play activities, drawing, painting, story telling, etc. Thus, without taking the subject to a private room for a clinical session, the observer can follow a child in a nursery school where he is channeled into various situations and given various materials, as part of the normal daily school program.

Under constructive methods may be grouped the active dramatic play with miniature life toys or any objects capable of being utilized as surrogates—symbols for actual life situations. Children and adults can be enlisted in a spontaneous dramatization of any theme or plot they may choose and in that dramatic play reveal what otherwise they could not or would not exhibit. Here we see the subject not only giving a projective configuration but investing the miniature life figures and setting with action, interpersonal relations and a dramatic plot with often a climax or abrupt termination when the action reaches a stage beyond the subject's ability to tolerate or handle such a dénouement.

Erik H. Erikson has remarked[3] that this abrupt, sudden interruption in play offers the most informing clues to the subject's hidden personality difficulties. Thus, it is not only the play configuration but the active manipulation and verbalizations of the subject which must be observed and interpreted as a whole sequence. Any single action or verbal statement must be seen and interpreted in the context of the subject's total production.

Rôle playing by the subject in concert with other living subjects, as in playing house or store or school, or in dramatizing various life situations, offers another opportunity to elicit from the subjects what they believe, think, feel and aspire to be. Thus, asking a small group of children to play house, each volunteering to be mother, father, baby, etc., and then observing how each plays that self-selected rôle reveals the individual's conception of these rôles, their own basic feelings toward parents, siblings, etc. Children will gladly play policeman, fireman, soldiers, and other rôles, each revealing his or her own personality in the interpretation of these rôles, as well as his understanding of these rôles.

The rôle playing of adults, as in psychodrama and sociodrama (Moreno), likewise provides opportunities for older subjects to reveal their otherwise concealed, disguised or unrecognized feelings and to discover potentialities they have never realized. Often the subjects need a "warming up" process to get into the rôles and to establish the appropriate mood. They may also need some active assistance to provoke their spontaneous rôle playing and release of spontaneous feelings, especially subjects who have long repressed their feelings or been burdened with persistent anxiety, guilt or resentful hostility.

Deliberate frustration of the subject's activities or desires may elicit reactions in play situations that are significant of various dimensions of the individual's personality process, especially when

[3] "Studies in Interpretation of Play," *Genet. Psychol. Monogr.*, 1940, 22, pp. 557-671.

he is given various materials (such as drawing, toys, etc.) to utilize for expressing his frustration. Here the subject reveals his capacity for accepting denials or frustration or his otherwise repressed hostility.

The use of therapeutic doll (David Levy) may be considered as partly a constructive method as well as a cathartic method (to be discussed later). In so far as the subject will manipulate the dolls and actively dramatize his own life situation, he is constructively using the dolls, revealing the configural pattern of interpersonal relations (to mother and to siblings). In so far as he may dismember the dolls and destructively release his chronic affective reactions, he may use the dolls for a catharsis of these feelings, which he has not dared to reveal otherwise. Here again clinical training and experience is necessary to know when and how to elicit these reactions and to help the child to learn to manage them for social living.

The therapeutic aim of releasing the subject from the constriction of strongly repressed feelings may be served by a variety of projective techniques. To the extent that the projective materials or situation offers the subject something to organize, manipulate, rearrange, interpret and even destroy, what he is given to use, he may gain a sense of mastery (Ives Hendrick) over the world, which otherwise is too refractory or frustrating or coercive for his own efforts to manage.

The danger of imputing to the child what may be more largely due to the value or character of the projective materials or situation should be obvious from watching children during the war playing with toy lethal weapons. Many children can release hostility-aggression, but some may find a source of added security, while others may be engaged in having a good time. The more the materials and the suggested play impose upon the subject a specific situation and either indicate or suggest (with clinician's verbal encouragement) any pattern of response, such as destructive hostility, the more careful must the clinician be in interpreting such a projection. Conversely, when the subject warps or distorts or converts any material or situation into an occasion for a patterned activity or expression of feeling not appropriate or usual to that situation or in such an activity, the more indicative it may be of his idiomatic personality.

INTERPRETATIVE METHODS

Since the individual learns early in life to conceal what he believes, thinks and how he feels on many aspects of life,[4] especially interpersonal relations, projective methods often make possible the revelation of what, as Murray has pointed out, "The subject cannot or will not say."

The interpretative methods offer the subject a situation or action to which he responds by a creative activity, wherein is disclosed his basic concepts, expectations, feelings.

Thus, in the Thematic Apperception Test and in variations thereon, the subject is shown a picture and asked to write or tell a story about the persons in that picture. This story may then be interpreted in various ways (such as Murray's press-need categories), according to the clinical significance given to the story as a whole and its various elements.

All creative literature is projective material, in and through which the writer is creating a fictional world expressive of his own personality makeup and affective reactions. He may be projecting what he hopes and desires or what he has rejected and is fleeing from. But, as indicated earlier, interpretation of a story must be exceedingly careful when unaccompanied by any other materials or life history. Context is essential to interpretive validity which means detailed "content analysis" or supporting materials from other projective materials.

The subject may be asked to react to a puppet show and to interpret the characters or dramatic action, including expression of his emotional reactions, as stimulated by the puppet play.

Simpler procedures include completion of unfinished sentences (expository or declarative) and of unfinished similes. Free association to a stimulus-situation, like music, chosen to arouse certain moods, also may be treated as interpretative responses.

In these interpretative procedures, we see the interrelation of clinical methods with the recently developed methods of *content*

[4] Cf. L. S. Vigotsky, "Thought and Speech," *Psychiatry*, 1939, 2, pp. 29-54.

analysis. In the latter, the content of any written production is subject to a more or less detailed anaylsis, from counting of words with different meanings, significance and symbolic use, to the identification of basic themes and patterns, of the underlying *eidos* and *ethos* of a culture. Content analysis, like opinion polls, reveals the traditional regularities of group life, the recurrently used images and sensibilities; while projective methods aim to disclose the idiomatic personality and how he uses these cultural patterns in his own individualized, often distorted, way, revealing his private world. The individual strives to maintain his private world within the limitations and opportunities of the public, cultural world. When the individual personality can no longer maintain communication with his fellows or can no longer meet the social requirements (denials and compulsions) of conduct, speech and expression of feelings, he may become psychotic, or turn to various anodynes, escapes and compensatory aids, such as crime, alcoholism, drugs, fantasy and other surrogates, benign or self-defeating, or socially destructive.

Interpretative methods may be combined with constitutive or constructive. Thus, the individual, having given a projective response, may be asked to interpret his own production—play configuration or the picture he has drawn, or other production. This may elicit, like the inquiry in Rorschach, more detailed information on the subject's private world as already revealed, or it may lead to further revelations and disclosures about that private world.

Interpretative methods may be distinguished from others by the emphasis upon the subject's individual way of giving meaning and significance to some presentation which is more or less structuralized, like a portrait, which is interpreted by each subject in a different way. As in all projective methods, there are more or less popular interpretations, the kind of generalized definitions given by many subjects, but even these will often vary in detailed expression or emphasis and context.

CATHARTIC METHODS

As indicated earlier, every projective method may stimulate some emotional reaction or elicit a chronic affective reaction, as it evokes the individual's persistent patterns of action, speech and thinking. But certain projective methods are especially effective in provoking emotions or releasing chronic feelings.

Perhaps the most frequent occurrence is at the theatre or "movies," where the members of the audience are in a favorable situation of darkness and a crowd, exposed to artistically created presentation designed to capture their personalities. We "identify" with the characters, that is, we accept their world, their problems and feelings as our own, temporarily putting aside our own pre-occupations while we live vicariously. Our chronic feelings of anxiety, of guilt and hostility are provided with a socially sanctioned, group shared, occasion for release. We see on the stage or screen others sharing our hopes and desires but often better able to translate them into overt words and actions and the fulfillment we may find difficult or impossible to achieve.

In projective cathartic methods the subject, as it were, has a dramatic experience and finds release for his feelings which brings a sense of liberation, at least for a time. Since, as children, we have been told we must not feel what we do feel (hate, aversion, fear, etc.) the opportunity to feel and express such forbidden or re-pressed feelings may provide clues to our affective capacities and anesthesias. Thus, these methods may be both diagnostic and ther-apeutic, often restoring the subject's spontaniety and providing outlet for expression.

The therapeutic doll (Levy), the use of clay modelling and its later destruction or distortion and similar manipulatible materials provide clinical methods for eliciting cathartic reactions.

The response to stories told by the clinician, particularly stories prepared especially to elicit emotional or affective reactions, also offers projective materials for understanding the individual per-sonality.

Observation of the subject's non-verbal reactions, hand, leg, facial gestures or tics, may be indicative of emotional releases un-der restraint by the subject.

REFRACTIVE METHODS

The use of any conventionalized mode of communication,

verbal or written, provides another approach to the subject's private world and idiomatic personality process.

Each person uses language in his own idiomatic way, with tones of voice, and other peculiarly formed expressions. Handwriting is also highly individualized, as each subject uses the common letters but differently written, in size, spacing, loops, symmetry or lack of symmetry, rhythms, and other characteristic expressions.

Almost all conventionalized patterns may be examined for the way the personality is transmitted, as through a lens, which, like the eye, refracts the light, combining, distorting, warping, bending, even eliminating, some parts of the pattern of light waves.

Just as the evidence of projective methods indicates that every sensation is a perception, a highly selective awareness and recognition, patterned by each personality, so it appears that each personality likewise converts each of our common expressive movements or sounds into a highly individualized, patterned mode of communication.

Thus, again, we may emphasize that there are recurrent, regular patterns, just as there are common ideas and sentiments, but for understanding the idiomatic personality, we must look for the individualized use of these patterns utilized by each personality in his own way, with his own meanings and intentions, his own emotional or affective coloring.

V
RELIABILITY AND VALIDITY OF PROJECTIVE METHODS

THE development of statistical methods for determining the reliability and validity of standardized tests some years ago has played a large rôle in the thinking and procedures of psychology, especially psychometrics.

The test has been conceived as an instrument for measuring the subject's conformity to or deviation from norms for age, sex and other groupings. It was necessary, therefore, to establish such norms or central tendencies by statistical manipulation of test findings on unknown subjects (i.e., subjects known only by age, sex and test responses). Each subject, therefore, was like the anonymous molecules in a gas, exhibiting a greater or less variation from the statistical pattern of regularity for that gas.

Since the subject was seen only once for the test and was unknown beyond name, age, sex, and perhaps another criterion for classification (e.g., race), it was of crucial importance to establish the reliability and the validity of each test by the only available methods, namely, statistical evaluations of the test findings when utilized by different examiners on similar *groups* of subjects and when compared with selected performance or other criteria for similar *groups* of subjects.

Reliability and validity, therefore, have been for *groups*, not individuals, each of whom is measured according to deviation from those *group* norms.

These criteria of reliability and validity are highly appropriate for standardized tests but are of doubtful applicability for projective methods, although some users of projective methods have earnestly tried to satisfy such criteria.

In projective methods, the examiner is not primarily concerned with the subject's deviations from a statistically established norm, which may or may not be significant. Especially in the study of personality development and of the personality process, such norms are of little significance and, indeed, may only obstruct investigation of such dynamic problems.

It is important to remember that the projective methods are for study of *identified individuals*, not anonymous units assumed to be alike except for quantitative variations from group norms. Moreover, these identified individuals are approached as unique configurations for which the projective method used must be reliable and valid in revealing that individual, identified personality. Thus, reliability and validity for a *group*, as generally established, have little significance, save for "screening" purposes.

Medicine has been confronted for a long time with the questions of validity and reliability which, however, could not be resolved by any ingenious statistical procedures. Medicine has to deal with *variability within the individual patient* whose structure, functions and activities are continually changing, from minute to minute, hour to hour, day to day and year by year. Medicine has had to practice *biological relativity* by exercising what is called clinical judgment. This has required the use of such concepts as the *syndrome* which permits the physician to recognize a recurrent pattern or configuration of disease when confronted with different patients with widely differing laboratory and other diagnostic findings, often quantitatively different but having the same relative significance for the same disease or disorder. It must not be forgotten that the individual patient's *variability* can never be neglected in clinical judgment.

The distortion or deformation of the generalized patterns of organic functions or anatomical organization or behavioral activity is significant, not the deviation of any single quantitative finding or single aberrant factor from a norm. Thus, cellular pathology looks for alterations in the total morphology and organization of cells and tissues, recognizing certain distortions as pathognomic. Likewise, internal medicine seeks to discover the disturbances in organic functions, the arhythmias, or dysfunctions of organ systems seen in the context of a total functioning organism-personality.[1] The hyperfunctioning or hypofunctioning or paradoxical functioning can be discovered only when seen in the total

[1] Cf. Roy G. Hoskins, *The Biology of Schizophrenia*, Norton, 1945.

clinical picture of the individual patient, although certain gross pathologies may be revealed sometimes by single diagnostic findings, as in a biopsy, of certain tissues, or abnormal content of excretions.

It is recognized that the individual subject-patient may give different responses to the same diagnostic procedure or projective method at different times and to different individual examiners. But these differences of response, which would be serious in a standardized test wherein each item is scored, rated or measured independently, are utilized to discover the subject's persistent patterns and dynamic processes. Such patterns and processes are revealed by these different responses which, nevertheless, are constellated by the individual in recurrent or persistent patterns.

It is just this relativistic interpretation which marks the shift from the older criteria of credibility based on quantitative similarities or identities to the newer criteria of equivalence of configural organization, as in stereochemistry, for example. By the former interpretation of quantitative chemistry, the presence of certain chemical elements in known quantitative amounts determined the nature of the compound; whereas today it is necessary to give a stereochemical formula which shows the molecular configuration, often with the same elements but spatially rearranged. Moreover, chemistry now recognizes that the same or equivalent dynamic chemical process may be found in a number of different reactions involving different chemical substances in different amounts but operating with the same basic process.

Chemistry took a great step forward when it began to think in terms of molecular configuration, as in the concept of the benzine ring. Psychology is now taking a similar step in recognizing personality configurations and perceptual patterning, as in Gestalt psychology and the recent work of the Dartmouth Eye Institute.[2]

Thus, reliability of projective methods, by the very nature of the method, involves the recognition of equivalent patterns and

[2] Adelbert Ames, Jr., "Binocular Vision as Affected by Relations between Uniocular Stimulus-Patterns in Commonplace Environments," *Am. J. Psychol.*, Vol. LIX, pp. 333-357.

of personality processes, as revealed by the use of a number of projective methods given to the same *identified* individual. The *congruence* of these several findings, which appears in the similarity or equivalence of patterns or processes, as revealed by the subject-patient to different examiners, indicates its reliability. There can be, and usually there are, obvious differences in each subject's responses, but these differences, even when quantified, do not invalidate the pattern or process.

As in many medical diagnostic tests, the interpretation of projective responses are often done "blind," without seeing the patient, just as most medical laboratory determinations are done "blind," without seeing the patient but are then brought together into a diagnostic or prognostic interpretation. Most standardized tests, especially the so-called objective tests, are also "blind," since the test is scored by someone who never sees the subject.

Validity of findings and of interpretations of projective methods is established by the corroboration of other findings, more especially by the clinical diagnosis of the subject-patient by psychiatrists who, like other physicians, operate with clinical methods and diagnostic categories and life histories. But projective methods rely chiefly upon *temporal* validation, that is, the corroborative evidence which accrues over time, as the individual personality is revealed at subsequent epochs in his life career.

Temporal validation has been utilized in various follow-up studies of projective methods and also in standardized tests such as the classic Genetic Studies of Genius and other longitudinal investigations.

Temporal validation may be either observational or experimental. In observational procedures the subject-patient is successively observed or examined after an interval of time, thereby revealing his persistent or consistent personality process for validating the earlier findings. In some cases projective findings on young preschool children have been obtained, while the child's personality was developing and while his "private world" was in process of organization. Thus, it has been possible to validate the projective productions of some children by reference to their actual home experiences, as in toilet training or the birth of a baby, the illness or death of the mother, or other traumatic events in the child's life.

Temporal validation has been carried out experimentally in studies where the subjects have been first exposed to experimental stresses or blocks and subsequently have exhibited their reactions to that experience in their projective productions, such as in the study of *Frustration and Regression* by Lewin, Barker, et al. But, it is obvious that such experimental procedures in temporal validation can be undertaken only when the personality is developing or emerging and so is susceptible to that experimental approach. This limits experimental procedures to the period before five or six and to the period in adolescence when the personality-private world may be undergoing the frequent stresses and strains of puberty and of post-pubertal reorientation to home and parents, to the other sex and to social life. Traumatic experiences abound in this epoch of life but little experimentation has been attempted to provide euphoric or constructive experiences, such as group work and group therapy.

Perhaps the most severe experimental studies involving temporal validation have been made using projective methods before and after shock therapy and surgical interference (e.g., prefrontal lobotomy). Operations for brain tumor have confirmed the diagnoses made by projective methods (Rorschach) while reliable medical diagnoses have corroborated the diagnoses by projective methods of various psychosomatic illness and disorders, such as peptic ulcer, hypertension, asthmas, arthritis, etc.

It may be pointed out that a strict application of psychometric criteria to clinical medicine, including most established laboratory and other diagnostic procedures, such as x-rays, would lead to the rejection of many of these methods which are daily being used to save the lives of individuals (including psychometrists!). At the same time it must be acknowledged that some clinical research, based upon examination or observation of a limited number of patients, suffers from failure to observe statistical standards, especially in the attempt to establish specific clinical "entities" and new diagnostic signs.

Various studies have attempted to demonstrate the lack of

validity of projective methods by showing that a projective screening test was not corroborated by the judgment of a group of psychologically naïve laymen (e.g., army officers whose rating of officer candidates differed from the screening results). These studies would be more impressive if they were temporally validated by a careful study of the subsequent life adjustments and performance of the officer candidates.

While psychologists customarily rely upon the judgment of lay, naïve individuals to validate their findings, it is difficult to find any scientific justification for such a procedure. If a scientific method or test is used, one cannot assume that the agreement or disagreement with its findings by a group of untrained, naïve judges (as in matching) has any significance. Yet, this reliance upon such judges is frequently cited as validating or invalidating a method.

The crucial point in questions of reliability and validity is the criteria of credibility involved.[3] So long as the criteria so highly developed for standardized tests on samples are accepted as required for all other procedures, it seems difficult, if not impossible, to resolve the current controversies. But when different criteria are recognized as appropriate for different procedures, such as use of signs or indicators, psychology can go forward, as physics has gone forward, utilizing different methods and criteria, according to the problem and the appropriate methodology, as in classical and quantum physics.

Recognition of this difficulty has led modern students of personality to search for *signs* rather than samples. The devices employed in the hope of eliciting signs by which the inner life of the individual may be unconsciously revealed are often grouped under the heading of projective methods.

But when we come to deal with what is often called the 'private world' of the individual, comprising as it does, the feelings, urges, beliefs, attitudes, and desires of which he may be dimly aware and which he is often reluctant to admit even to himself, much less to others, the problems of measurement are of a very different nature. Here the universe we wish to assay is no longer overt and accessible but covert and

---

[3] Cf. Helen Sargent, "Projective Methods," *Psychol. Bull.*, Vol. 42, No. 5, May, 1945. See especially page 275, "Methodological Problems."

jealously guarded. Thus, the methods of direct sampling become hazardous since an unbiased sampling is so difficult to secure.[4]

It is probable that the foregoing discussion will appear "Incompetent, irrelevant and immaterial," as the legal phraseology expresses it, to those who have spent their professional lives on the laborious tasks of developing standardized, quantitative methods. Many feel that projective methods threaten scientific psychology. It may allay their anxiety to point out that projective methods and these unorthodox criteria of reliability and validity are not offered as superseding psychometric techniques and tests.

What is proposed is that projective methods be accepted as a promising development for the study of problems which have been elusive or baffling when approached by the accepted assumptions and customary methods. If the younger students are permitted to try these new concepts and to explore these newer procedures without risking their professional standing in the eyes of their elders, projective methods, *as a procedure*, will inevitably be temporally validated or, more probably, develop into scientifically acceptable methods, as judged by the emerging new criteria of credibility.

[4] Florence L. Goodenough, "Semantic Choice and Personality Structure," *Science*, Vol. 104, No. 2717, November 15, 1945.

APPENDIX

The term *projective methods* was first publicly used by the writer in a paper given before the Section of Psychology of the New York Academy of Sciences, May 15, 1939. It was earlier used by the writer in a privately circulated memorandum in 1938, from which came the title of a paper, "Projective Methods in the Psychological Study of Children," by Ruth Horowitz and Lois Barclay Murphy (*J. Exper. Educ.*, Vol. 7, No. 2, December, 1938).

As stated in the 1939 Academy paper:

It may be emphasized that projective methods are not offered as a substitute for the quantitative statistical procedures, but rather are designed to permit a study of the unique idiomatic individual which is conceived as a process of organizing experience and so must elude the investigator who relies upon methods that of necessity ignore or obscure the individual and the configural quality of his personality. Finally it should be noted that projective methods of personality study offer possibilities for utilizing the insights into human conduct and personality expression which the prevailing quantitative procedures seem deliberately to ignore.

Transactions, N. Y. Academy of Sciences
Series II, Vol. 1, No. 8. June 1939.

PARTIAL BIBLIOGRAPHY OF PROJECTIVE METHODS

Drawn in part from Helen Sargent's paper, "Projective Methods: Their Origins, Theory, and Application in Personality Research."

SECTION I. PROJECTIVE METHODOLOGY

BALKEN, EVA RUTH. Projective techniques for the study of personality. A critique. *Psychol. Bull.*, 1941, 38, 596. (Abstract.)

BELLAK, LEOPOLD. "The Concept of Projection." *Psychiatry*, 1944, 7, 353-70.

BROWN, J. F. & RAPAPORT, D. The role of the psychologist in the psychiatric clinic. *Bull. Menninger Clin.*, 1941, 5, 75-84.

BOOTH, GEORGE C. Objective techniques in personality testing. *Arch. Neurol. & Psychiat.*, Chicago, 1939, 42, 514-530.

FEIGENBAUM, D. On projection. *Psychoanalyt. Quart.*, 1936, 5, 303-319.

FRANK, L. K. Projective methods for the study of personality. *J. Psychol.*, 1939, 8, 389-413. (Also in *Tr. N. Y. Acad. Sci.*, 1939, 1, 129-132.)

FREUD, SIGMUND. *The Poet and Daydreaming.* Collected papers, Vol. 4. London: Hogarth Press, 1925.

GOODENOUGH, FLORENCE L. Semantic choice and personality structure. *Science*, 1946, 104, 451-456.

HOROWICZ, RUTH, & MURPHY, LOIS. Projective methods in the psychological study of children. *J. Exp. Educ.*, 1938, 7, 133-140.

KENDIG, ISABELLE. "Projective Technics as a Psychological Tool in Diagnosis." *J. Clin. Psychopathol.*, 1944, 7, 101-10.

LERNER, E., MURPHY, LOIS, STONE, L. J., BEYER, EVELYN, & BROWN, ELINOR. Studying child personality. *Monogr. Soc. Res. Child Develpm.*, 1941, 6, No. 4.

LEVINSON, DANIEL J. A note on the similarities and differences between projective tests and ability tests. *Psychol. Rev.*, 1946, 53, 189-194.

MacFARLANE, J. W. Critique of projective techniques. *Psychol. Bull.*, 1941, 38, 746.

MacFARLANE, J. W. Problems of validation inherent in projective methods. *Am. J. Orthopsychiat.*, 1942, 12, 405-411.

MASLOW, A. H. & MITTELMANN, B. *Principles of Abnormal Psychology*. Appendix I. Projective methods of examination. Pp. 611-622. New York: Harper, 1941.

MOELLENHOFF, F. A projection returns and materializes. *Am. Imago*, 1942, 3, 3-13.

MURPHY, LOIS B. Interiorization of family experiences by normal preschool children as revealed by some projective methods. *Psychol. League J.*, 1940, 4, 3-5.

MURPHY, LOIS B. Patterns of spontaneity and constraint in the use of projective materials by preschool children. *Tr. N. Y. Acad. Sci.*, 1942, 4, 124-138.

MURPHY, LOIS B. *Social Behavior and Child Personality. An exploratory study of some roots of sympathy*. New York: Columbia Univ. Press, 1937.

MURRAY, H. A. Effect of fear on estimates of maliciousness of other personalities. *In* Tomkins, Silvan S. *Contemporary Psychopathology*. Cambridge: Harvard Univ. Press, 1943. Pp. 545-561.

MURRAY, H. A. *Explorations in Personality*. New York: Oxford Univ. Press, 1938.

MURRAY, H. A. An investigation of fantasies. *In* Abstract of C. L. Hull's informal seminar at Yale University, 1936. (Unpublished.)

RAPAPORT, D. *Diagnostic psychological testing: the theory, statistical evaluation, and diagnostic application of a battery of tests*. Chicago: Year Book Publishers, 1946. Menninger Clin. Monogr., Series No. 4, Vol. II.

RAPAPORT, D. Principles underlying projective techniques. *Character & Pers.*, 1942, 10, 213-219.

REICHENBERG, W. & CHIDESTER, LEONA. Lack of imagination as a factor in delinquent behavior. *Bull. Menninger Clin.*, 1937, 1, 226-231.

ROSENZWEIG, S. Fantasy in personality and its study by test procedures. *J. Abnorm. & Soc. Psychol.*, 1942, 37, 40-51.

SARGENT, HELEN. Projective methods: their origins, theory and application in personality research. *Psychol. Bull.*, 1945, 42, 257-293.

SEARS, R. R. Experimental studies of projection: I. Attribution of traits. *In* Tomkins, Silvan S. *Contemporary Psychopathology*. Cambridge: Harvard Univ. Press, 1943. Pp. 561-571.

STRANG, RUTH. Technical instruments of mental hygiene diagnosis and therapy. *Rev. Educ. Res.*, 1940, 10, 450-459.

SYMONDS, P. M. & SAMUEL, E. A. Projective methods in the study of personality. *Rev. Educ. Res.*, 1941, 11, 80-93.

UPDEGRAFF, RUTH. Recent approaches to the study of the preschool child. I. Indirect and projective methods. *J. Consult. Psychol.*, 1938, 2, 159-161.

WHITE, R.W. The interpretation of imaginative productions. *In* Hunt, J. McV. *Personality and the Behavior Disorders. A handbook based on experimental research.* (2 vol.) New York: Ronald Press, 1944, pp. 214-254.

WOLFF, W. Projective methods for personality analysis of expressive behavior in preschool children. *Character & Pers.*, 1942, 10, 309-330.

WOLFF, WERNER. *The Personality of the Preschool Child.* New York: Grune & Stratton, 1946.

SECTION II. SPECIAL METHODS

Art Techniques

ABEL, THEODORA M. Free designs of limited scope as a personality index. *Character & Pers.*, 1938, 7, 50-62.

ALSCHULER, ROSE H. & HATTWICK, LA BERTA WEISS. *Painting and Personality. A study of young children.* Chicago: Univ. Chicago Press, 1947.

ALSCHULER, ROSE H., AND HATTWICK, LA BERTA WEISS. "Easel Painting as an Index of Personality in Preschool Children." *Am. J. Orthopsychiat.*, 1943, 13, 616-25.

ANASTASI, A. & FOLEY, J. P. A survey of the literature on artistic behavior in the abnormal: III. Spontaneous productions. *Psychol. Monogr.*, 1942, 52, No. 237.

ARLOW, JACOB A., AND KADIS, ASJA. "Finger Painting in the Psychotherapy of Children." *Am. J. Orthopsychiat.*, 1946, 16, 134-36.

BARNHART, E. N. Stages in construction of children's drawing as revealed through a recording device. *Psychol. Bull.*, 1940, 37, 581. (Abstract.)

BEACH, VERA & BRESSLER, MARY H. Organizing a painting set-up for young children. *J. Exper. Educ.*, 1944, 13, 78-80.

BENDER, LAURETTA. Art and therapy in the mental disturbances of children. *J. Nerv. & Ment. Dis.*, 1937, 86, 249-263.

BENDER, LAURETTA. Gestalt principles in the side-walk drawings and games of children. *J. Genet. Psychol.*, 1932, 41, 192-210.

BENDER, LAURETTA. The Goodenough test in chronic encephalitis in children. *J. Nerv. & Ment. Dis.*, 1940, 91, 277-286.

BENDER, LAURETTA & WOLTMANN, A. G. The use of plastic material as a psychiatric approach to emotional problems of children. *Am. J. Orthopsychiat.*, 1937, 7, 283-300.

BENDER, LAURETTA, AND RAPAPORT, JACK. "Animal Drawings of Children." *Am. J. Orthopsychiat.*, 1944, 14, 521-27.

BRICK, MARIA. "Mental Hygiene Value of Children's Art Work." *Am. J. Orthopsychiat.*, 1944, 14, 136-46.

ELKISCH, PAULA. Children's drawings in a projective technique. *Psychol. Monogr.*, 1945, 58, 1-31.

FLEMING, J. Observations on the use of finger painting in the treatment of adult patients with personality disorders. *Character & Pers.*, 1940, 8, 301-310.

HARMS, E. Child art as an aid in the diagnosis of juvenile neuroses. *Am. J. Orthopsychiat.*, 1941, 11, 191-209.

HURLOCK, ELIZABETH B. "The Spontaneous Drawings of Adolescents." *J. Genet. Psychol.*, 1943, 63, 141-56.

LEVY, J. Use of art techniques in treatment of children's behavior problems. *Proc. Am. A. Ment. Deficiency*, 1934, 58, 258-260.

LEWIS, N. D. C. Graphic art productions in schizophrenia. *Proc. A. Res. Nerv. & Ment. Dis.*, 1928, 5, 344-368.

LISS, E. The graphic arts. *Am. J. Orthopsychiat.*, 1938, 8, 95-99.

McINTOSH, J. R. An inquiry into the use of children's drawings as a means of psychoanalysis. *Brit. J. Educ. Psychol.*, 1939, 9, 102-103. (Abstract.)

McINTOSH, J. R. & PICKFORD, R. W. Some clinical and artistic aspects of a child's drawings. *Brit. J. M. Psychol.*, 1943, 19, 342-362.

MOSSE, E. P. Painting analysis in the treatment of neuroses. *Psychoanalyt. Rev.*, 1940, 27, 68-82.

NAPOLI, PETER J. Finger-painting and personality diagnosis. *Genet. Psychol. Monogr.*, 1946, 129-231.

NAPOLI, PETER J. Interpretive aspects of finger-painting. *J. Psychol.*, 1947, 23, 93-132.

NAUMBERG, M. Children's art expressions and war. *Nerv. Child*, 1943, 2, 360-373.

NAUMBERG, MARGARET. "A Study of the Art Expression of a Behavior Problem Boy as an Aid in Diagnosis and Therapy." *Nerv. Child*, 1944, 3, 277-319.

NAUMBERG, MARGARET. Free art expression of behavior problem children and adolescents. *Nerv. & Ment. Dis. Monogr.*, 1947.

REITMAN, F. Facial expression in schizophrenic drawing. *J. Ment. Sc.*, 1939, 85, 264-272.

SCHMIEDL, WAEHNER, T. Formal criteria for the analysis of children's drawing. *Am. J. Orthopsychiat.*, 1942, 12, 95-104.

SCHUBE, K. & COWELL, G. Art of psychotic persons. *Arch. Neurol. & Psychiat.*, 1939, 41, 709-720.

SHAW, RUTH F. *Finger Painting.* Little Brown, Boston, 1934.

SHAW, RUTH F. & LYLE, JEANNETTE. Encouraging fantasy expression in children. *Bull. Menninger Clin.*, 1937, 1, 78-86.

SPOERL, D. T. Personality and drawing in retarded children. *Character & Pers.*, 1940, 8, 227-239.

SPRINGER, N. N. A study of the drawings of maladjusted and adjusted children. *J. Genet. Psychol.*, 1941, 58, 131-138.

WAEHNER, TRUDE S. "Interpretation of Spontaneous Drawings and Paintings." *Genetic Psychology Monogr.*, 1946, 33, 1-70.

WILLIAMS, J. N. Interpretation of drawings made by maladjusted children. *Virg., Med. Monogr.*, 1940, 67, 533-538.

Drama and Puppets

BENDER, LAURETTA & WOLTMANN, A. Puppetry as a psychotherapeutic measure with problem children. *Bull., N. Y. State A. Occup. Therap.*, 1937, 7, 1-7.

BENDER, LAURETTA & WOLTMANN, A. G. The use of puppet shows as a psychotherapeutic method for behavior problems in children. *Am. J. Orthopsychiat.*, 1936, 6, 341-354.

BORDIN, RUTH. The use of psychodrama in an institute for delinquent girls. *Sociometry*, 1940, 3, 80-90.

CURRAN, FRANK J. The drama as a therapeutic measure in adolescence. *Am. J. Orthopsychiat.*, 1939, 9, 215-232.

FRANZ, J. G. The place of the psychodrama in research. *Sociometry*, 1940, 3, 49-61.

JENKINS, R. L. & BECKH, E. Finger puppets and mask making as a media for work with children. *Am. J. Orthopsychiat.*, 1942, 12, 294-301.

LYLE, J. & HOLLY, S. B. The therapeutic value of puppets. *Bull. Menninger Clin.*, 1941.

MORENO, J. L. Mental catharsis and the psychodrama. *Sociometry*, 1940, 3, 209-244.

MORENO, J. L. Psychodramatic shock therapy. A sociometric approach to the problem of mental disorders. *Sociometry*, 1939, 2, 1-30.

WOLTMANN, A. G. The use of puppets in understanding children. *Ment. Hyg.*, 1940, 24, 445-458.

Graphology

BOOTH, G. C. The use of graphology in medicine. *J. Nerv. & Ment. Dis.*, 1937, 86, 674-679.

EYSENCK, H. J. Graphological analysis and psychiatry: an experimental study. *Brit. J. Psychol.*, 1945, 35, 70-81.

GOODENOUGH, F. L. Sex differences in judging the sex of handwriting. *J. Social Psychol.*, 1945, 22, 61-68.

MARUM, O. Character assessment from handwriting. *J. Ment. Sc.*, 1945, 91, 22-42.

PASCAL, G. R. Handwriting pressure: its measurement and significance. *Character & Pers.*, 1943, 11, 235-254.

PASCAL, G. R. The analysis of handwriting; a test of significance. *Character & Pers.*, 1943, 12, 123-144.

SCHRYVER, S. Psychomotility in behavior disorders as seen in the handwriting of children. *J. Nerv. & Ment. Dis.*, 1944, 100, 64-69.

STEIN-LEWINSON, THEA. An introduction to the graphology of Ludwig Klages. *Character & Pers.*, 1938, 6, 163-177.

SUPER, D. E. A comparison of the diagnoses of a graphologist with the results of psychological tests. *J. Consult. Psychol.*, 1941, 5, 127-133.

WELLS, F. L. Personal history, handwriting, and specific behavior. *J. Pers.*, 1946, 14, 295-314.

Play Techniques

ACKERMAN, N. W. Constructive and destructive tendencies in children. *Am. J. Orthopsychiat.*, 1937, 7, 301-319.

ACKERMAN, N. W. Constructive and destructive tendencies in children. An experimental study. *Am. J. Orthopsychiat.*, 1938, 8, 265-285.

ALLEN, F. H. *Psychotherapy with Children.* New York, W. W. Norton, 1942.

ALLEN, F. H. Therapeutic work with children. *Am. J. Orthopsychiat.*, 1934, 4, 193-202.

ANDERSON, H. H. Domination and integration in the social behavior of young children in an experimental play situation. *Genet. Psychol. Monogr.*, 1937, 19, 343-408.

BACH, G. R. Young children's play fantasies. *Psychol. Monogr.*, 1945, 59, No. 2.

BARUCH, DOROTHY W. Aggression during doll play in a preschool. *Am. J. Orthopsychiat.*, 1941, 11, 252-260.

BARUCH, DOROTHY W. Play techniques in pre-school as an aid in guidance. *Psychol. Bull.*, 1939, 36, 570. (Abstract.)

BENDER, LAURETTA, & SCHILDER, P. Aggressiveness in children. *Genet. Psychol. Monogr.*, 1936, 18, 410-525.

BENDER, LAURETTA & SCHILDER, P. Form as a principle in the play of children. *J. Genet. Psychol.*, 1936, 49, 254-261.

CAMERON, W. M. The treatment of children in psychiatric clinics with particular reference to the use of play techniques. *Bull. Menninger Clin.*, 1940, 4, 172-180.

CONN, J. H. The child reveals himself through play. *Ment. Hyg.*, 1939, 23, 49-69.

CONN, J. H. The play interview. A method of studying children's attitudes. *Am. J. Dis. Child.*, 1939, 58, 1199-1214.

CONN, J. H. A psychiatric study of car sickness in children. *Am. J. Orthopsychiat.*, 1938, 8, 130-141.

DESPERT, J. LOUISE. A method for the study of personality reactions in pre-school age children by means of analysis of their play. *J. Psychol.*, 1940, 9, 17-29.

DESPERT, J. LOUISE. Technical approaches used in the study of emotional problems in children. Part IV. Collective phantasy. *Psychiat. Quart.*, 1937, 11, 491-506.

DESPERT, J. LOUISE. Technical approaches used in the study of emotional problems in children. Part V. The playroom. *Psychiat. Quart.*, 1937, 11, 677-693.

ERIKSON, ERIK HOMBURGER. Configurations in play. Clinical notes. *Psychoanal. Quart.*, 1937, 6, 139-214.

ERIKSON, E. H. Dramatic productions test. *In* Murray, H. A., et al. *Explorations in Personality.* New York: Oxford, 1938, 552-582.

ERIKSON, ERIK HOMBURGER. Further explorations in play construction. Three spatial variables in relation to sex and anxiety. *Psychol. Bull.*, 1938, 41, 748. (Abstract.)

ERIKSON, ERIK HOMBURGER. Studies in the interpretation of play. Clinical observations of play disruption in young children. *Genet. Psychol. Monogr.*, 1940, 22, 557-671.

FREUD, ANNA. Introduction to the technique of child analysis. (Authorized trans. supervised by L. P. Clark.) *Nerv. & Ment. Dis. Monogr.*, 1928, No. 48.

FRIES, MARGARET E. Play technique in the analysis of young children. *Psychoanal. Rev.*, 1937, 24, 233-245.

FRIES, MARGARET E. The value of play for a child development study. *Understand. Child*, 1938, 7, 15-18.

GITELSON, M. Clinical experience with play therapy. *Am. J. Orthopsychiat.*, 1938, 8, 466-478.

GITELSON, M., ROSS, H., HOMBURGER, E., ALLEN, F., BLANCHARD, PHYLLIS, LIPPMAN, H. S., GERARD, M. & LOWERY, L. Section on play therapy. *Am. J. Orthopsychiat.*, 1938, 8, 499-524.

HENRY, J., AND HENRY, Z. *Doll Play of Pilaga Indian Children.* Research Monograph of the American Orthopsychiatric Association, No. 4. New York, 1944. 133 pp.

HOLMER, P. The use of the play situation as an aid to diagnosis. A case report. *Am. J. Orthopsychiat.*, 1937, 7, 523-531.

KANNER, LEO. Play investigations and play treatment of children's behavior disorders. *J. Pediat.*, 1940, 17, 533-545.

KLEIN, MELANIE. *The Psychoanalysis of Children.* London: Hogarth Press, 1932.

LEVY, D. Hostility patterns in sibling rivalry experiments. *Am. J. Orthopsychiat.*, 1936, 6, 183-257.

LEVY, D. Release therapy in young children. *Psychiat.*, 1938, 1, 387-390.

LEVY, D. Studies in sibling rivalry. *Res. Monogr. Am. Orthopsychiat. A.*, 1937, No. 2.

LEVY, D. Use of play technique as experimental procedure. *Am. J. Orthopsychiat.*, 1933, 3, 266-277.

LISS, E. Play techniques in child analysis. *Am. J. Orthopsychiat.*, 1936, 6, 17-22.

LOWENFELD, MARGARET. The theory and use of play in the psychotherapy of childhood. *J. Ment. Sc.*, 1938, 84, 1057-1058.

MAYER, A. M. & MAYER, E. B. Dynamic concept test. A modified play technique for adults. *Psychiat. Quart.*, 1941, 15, 621-634.

NEWELL, H. W. Play therapy in child psychiatry. *Am. J. Orthopsychiat.*, 1941, 11, 245-252.

PHILLIPS, R. Doll play as a function of the realism of the materials and the length of the experimental session. *Child Devel.*, 1945, 16, 123-143.

PINTLER, M. H., PHILLIPS, R. & SEARS, R. R. Sex differences in the projective doll play of pre-school children. *J. Psychol.*, 1946, 21, 73-80.

RICHARDS, S. S. & WOLFF, E. The organization and function of play activities in the set-up of a pediatrics department. *Ment. Hyg., N. Y.*, 1940, 24, 229-235.

ROBINSON, ELIZABETH F. Doll play as a function of the doll family constellation. *Child Devel.*, 1946, 17, 99-119.

ROGERSON, C. H. *Play Therapy in Childhood.* New York: Oxford Univ. Press, 1939.

ROSENZWEIG, S. & SHAKOW, D. Play technique in schizophrenia and other psychoses: I. Rationale; II. An experimental study of schizophrenic constructions with play materials. *Am. J. Orthopsychiat.*, 1937, 7, 32-35; 36-47.

SARGENT, HELEN D. Spontaneous doll play of a nine-year-old. *J. Consult. Psychol.*, 1943, 7, 216-222.

SIMPSON, G. Diagnostic play interviews. *Understand. Child*, 1938, 7, 6-10.

SOLOMON, J. C. Active play therapy. *Am. J. Orthopsychiat.*, 1938, 8, 479-498.

SOLOMON, J. C. Active play therapy. Further experiences. *Am. J. Orthopsychiat.*, 1940, 10, 763-781.

SYMONDS, P. M. Play technique as a test of readiness. *Understand. Child*, 1940, 9, 8-14.

TALLMAN, F. & GOLDENSOHN, L. N. Play techniques. *Am. J. Orthopsychiat.*, 1941, 11, 551-561.

WALDER, R. The psychoanalytic theory of play. *Psychoanal. Quart.*, 1933, 2, 208-224.

WEISS-FRANKL, A. B. Diagnostic and remedial play. *Understand. Child*, 1938, 7, 3-5.

YARROW, L. *The Effect of Frustration of Doll Fantasy Behavior.* Ph.D. thesis. State University of Iowa, 1946.

Rorschach Method

BECK, S. J. Autism in Rorschach scoring: a feeling comment. *Character & Pers.*, (News and Notes), 1936, 5, 83-85.

BECK, S. J. Configurational tendencies in Rorschach responses. *Am. J. Psychol.*, 1933, 45, 433-443.

BECK, S. J. Error, symbol and method in the Rorschach test. *J. Abnorm. & Social Psychol.*, 1942, 37, 83-103.

BECK, S. J. Introduction to the Rorschach method. A manual of personality study. *Res. Monogr. Am. Orthopsychiat. A.*, 1937, No. 1.

BECK, S. J. Personality structure in schizophrenia. A Rorschach investigation on 81 patients and 64 controls. *Nerv. & Ment. Dis. Monogr.*, 1938, No. 63.

BECK, S. J. Psychological processes in Rorschach findings. *J. Abnorm. & Social Psychol.*, 1937, 31, 482-488.

BECK, S. J. The Rorschach test in psychopathology. *J. Consult. Psychol.*, 1943, 7, 103-111.

BECK, S. J. *Rorschach's Test.* I: Elementary principles. New York: Grune & Stratton, 1944.

BECK, S. J. *Rorschach's Test.* II: A Variety of Personality Pictures. New York: Grune and Stratton, 1945. 402 pp.

BENJAMIN, J. A. & EBAUGH, F. G. The diagnostic validity of the Rorschach test. *Am. J. Psychiat.*, 1938, 94, 1163-1178.

BINDER, H. The "light-dark" interpretations in Rorschach's experiment. *Rorschach Res. Exch.*, 1937, 2, 37-42.

BOCHNER, RUTH & HALPERN, FLORENCE. *Clinical Application of the Rorschach Test.* New York: Grune & Stratton, 1942.

BRENMAN, MARGARET & REICHARD, SUZANNE. Use of the Rorschach test in the prediction of hypnotizability. *Bull. Menninger Clin.*, 1943, 7, 183-188.

FOSBERG, I. An experimental study of the reliability of the Rorschach psycho-diagnostic technique. *Rorschach Res. Exch.*, 1941, 5, 72-84.

FRANK, L. K. Foreword to issue on the Rorschach method. *J. Consult. Psychol.*, 1943, 7, 63-66.

GOLDFARB, WILLIAM. "Organization Activity in the Rorschach Examination." *Am. J. Orthopsychiat.*, 15: 525-28; July 1945.

HALLOWELL, A. IRVING. "The Rorschach Technic in the Study of Personality and Culture." *American Anthropologist*, 47: 195-210; April-June 1945.

HARROWER, MOLLY R. *Psycho-diagnostic Inkblots*. Manual and ten plates. New York: Grune and Stratton, 1945.

HARROWER-ERICKSON, MOLLY R. The contribution of the Rorschach method to war-time psychological problems. *J. Ment. Sci.*, 1940, 86, 1-12.

HARROWER-ERICKSON, MOLLY R. Large scale experimentation with the Rorschach method. *J. Consult. Psychol.*, 1943, 7, 120-127.

HARROWER-ERICKSON, MOLLY R., AND STEINER, MATHILDA E. *Large Scale Rorschach Techniques*. Springfield, Illinois: Thomas, 1945.

HARROWER-ERICKSON, MOLLY R. Modification of the Rorschach method for use as a group test. *Rorschach Res. Exch.*, 1941, 5, 130-144.

HARROWER-ERICKSON, MOLLY R. Personality Changes accompanying Cerebral Lesions, I. Rorschach Studies of Patients with Cerebral Tumors. *Arch. Neurol. & Psychiat.*, 1940, 43, 859-890.

HARROWER-ERICKSON, MOLLY R. Personality Changes accompanying Cerebral Lesions, II. Rorschach Studies of Patients with Focal Epilepsy. *Arch. Neurol. & Psychiat.*, 1940, 43, 1081-1107.

HARROWER-ERICKSON, MOLLY R. Personality Changes accompanying Organic Brain Lesions, III. A Study of Pre-Adolescent Children. *J. Genet. Psychol.*, 1941, 58, 391-405.

HARROWER-ERICKSON, MOLLY R. Psychological Studies in Patients with Epileptic Seizures. Chapter IX in *Epilepsy and Cerebral Localization* by Wilder Penfield and Theodore C. Erickson. Springfield, Illinois: Thomas, 1941.

HARROWER-ERICKSON, MOLLY R. The Patient and his Personality. *McGill M. J.*, 1941, XI, No. 1, 25-40.

HARROWER-ERICKSON, MOLLY R. Clinical Use of Psychological Tests. *McGill M. J.*, 1941, XI, No. 2, 105-109.

HARROWER-ERICKSON, MOLLY R. Diagnosis of Psychogenic factors in disease by Means of the Rorschach method. *Psychiat. Quart.*, 1943, 17, 57-66.

HARROWER-ERICKSON, MOLLY R. A Multiple Choice Test for Screening Purposes (for use with Rorschach cards or slides). *Psychosom. Med.*, 1943, V, No. 4, 331-341.

HARROWER-ERICKSON, MOLLY R. The Rorschach Method in the Study of Personality. *Ann. N. Y. Acad. Sci.*, 1943, XLIV, Art. 6, December 22, 569-588.

HARROWER-ERICKSON, MOLLY R. The Rorschach Test. *J. A. Am. M. Coll.*, 1944, pp. 1-8.

HERTZ, MARGUERITE R. Comparison of three blind Rorschach analyses. *Am. J. Orthopsychiat.*, 1939, 9, 295-315.

HERTZ, MARGUERITE R. Rorschach twenty years after. *Psychol. Bull.*, 1942, 39, 529-572.

HERTZ, MARGUERITE R. Scoring the Rorschach test with specific reference to the normal detail category. *Am. J. Orthopsychiat.*, 1938, 8, 100-121.

HERTZ, MARGUERITE R. The method of administration of the Rorschach ink blot test. *Child Devel.*, 1936, 7, 237-254.

HERTZ, MARGUERITE R. *Frequency Tables to be Used in Scoring the Rorschach Inkblot Test.* Cleveland: Brush Foundation, Western Reserve, 1936.

HERTZ, MARGUERITE R. The shading response in the Rorschach inkblot test: a review of its scoring and interpretation. *J. Gen. Psychol.*, 1940, 23, 123-167.

HERTZ, MARGUERITE R. The Rorschach method: science or mystery. *J. Consult. Psychol.*, 1943, 7, 67-80.

HERTZ, MARGUERITE R. Validity of the Rorschach method. *Am. J. Orthopsychiat.*, 1941, 11, 512-520.

HERTZ, MARGUERITE R. *The Rorschach Psychogram.* Revision 1946. Cleveland, Ohio: Dept. of Psychology, Western Reserve University. 1946.

HERTZ, MARGUERITE R., AND EBERT, ELIZABET H. "The Mental Procedure of Six and Eight-Year-Old Children as Revealed by the Rorschach Inkblot Method." *Rorschach Res. Exch.*, 1944, 8, 10-30.

HERTZ, MARGUERITE R. & RUBENSTEIN, B. B. A comparison of three "blind" Rorschach analyses. *Am. J. Orthopsychiat.*, 1939, 9, 295-314.

HERTZMANN, M. Recent research on the group Rorschach test. *Rorschach Res. Exch.*, 1943, 7, 1-6.

HERTZMANN, M. & MARGULIES, HELEN. Developmental changes in Rorschach test responses. *J. Genet. Psychol.*, 1943, 62, 189-216.

HUNTER, MARY. The practical value of the Rorschach test in a psychological clinic. *Am. J. Orthopsychiat.*, 1939, 9, 287-294.

KAMMAN, GORDON R. "The Rorschach Method as a Therapeutic Agent." *Am. J. Orthopsychiat.*, 1944, 14, 21-28.

KELLEY, D. M. The present state of the Rorschach method as a psychological adjunct. *Rorschach Res. Exch.*, 1940, 4, 30-36.

KELLEY, D. M. & KLOPFER, B. Application of the Rorschach method to research in schizophrenia. *Rorschach Res. Exch.*, 1939, 3, 55-66.

KISKER, G. W. A projective approach to personality patterns during insul shock and metrazol convulsive therapy. *J. Abnorm. & Social Psychol.*, 1942, 37, 120-124.

KLOPFER, BRUNO, AND DAVIDSON, HELEN H. *The Rorschach Technic*, 1946 Supplement. Yonkers, N. Y.: World Book Co., 1946. p. 431-75.

KLOPFER, B. & KELLEY, D. *The Rorschach Technique.* Yonkers, N. Y.: World, 1942.

KRUGMAN, J. E. A clinical validation of the Rorschach with problem children. *Rorschach Res. Exch.*, 1942, 6, 61-70.

KRUGMAN, M. The Rorschach in child guidance. *J. Consult. Psychol.*, 1943, 7, 80-88.

KRUGMAN, M. Out of the inkwell: the Rorschach method. *Character & Pers.*, 1940, 9, 91-110.

MIALE, F. R., CLAPP, H., & KAPLAN, A. H. Clinical validation of a Rorschach interpretation. *Rorschach Res. Exch.*, 1938, 2, 153-163.

MUNROE, RUTH. An experiment in large scale testing by a modification of the Rorschach method. *J. Psychol.*, 1942, 13, 229-263.

MUNROE, RUTH. The inspection technique. A modification of the Rorschach method of personality diagnosis for large scale application. *Rorschach Res. Exch.*, 1941, 5, 166-190.

MUNROE, RUTH. Use of the Rorschach in college counseling. *J. Consult. Psychol.*, 1943, 7, 89-97.

MUNROE, RUTH L. Prediction of the Adjustment and Academic Performance of College Students by a Modification of the Rorschach Method. *Applied Psychology Monographs*, No. 7. Stanford University, Calif.: Stanford University Press, 1945. 104 pp.

MUNROE, RUTH L. "The Rorschach Test: a Report of Its Use at Sarah Lawrence College." Journal of Higher Education, 1945, 16, 17-23.

OBERHOLZER, E. Rorschach's experiment and the Alorese. *In* DuBois, Cora, *The People of Alor.* Minneapolis, Univ. Minnesota Press, 1944.

PIOTROWSKI, Z. Blind analysis of a case of compulsion neurosis. *Rorschach Res. Exch.*, 1937, 2, 89-111.

PIOTROWSKI, Z. The *M, FM* and *m* responses as indicators of changes in personality. *Rorschach Res. Exch.*, 1937, 1, 148-156.

PIOTROWSKI, Z. The methodological aspects of the Rorschach personality method. *Kwart. Psychol.*, at Poznan, 1937, 9, 29.

PIOTROWSKI, Z. Use of the Rorschach in vocational selection. *J. Consult. Psychol.*, 1943, 7, 97-102.

PIOTROWSKI, ZYGMUNT A., AND OTHERS. "Rorschach Signs in the Selection of Outstanding Young Male Mechanical Workers." *J. Psychol.*, 1944, 18, 131-50.

RICKERS-OVSIANKINA, M. Rorschach scoring samples. Worcester, Massachusetts: Worcester State Hospital, 1938.

RORSCHACH, H. *Psychodiagnostics: A Diagnostic Test Based on Perception.* (Trans. by P. Lemkau & B. Kronenburg.) Bern, Hans Huber, 1942. New York: Grune and Stratton.

RORSCHACH, H. & OBERHOLZER, E. The application of the interpretation of form to psychoanalysis. *J. Nerv. & Ment. Dis.*, 1924, 60, 225-248; 359-379.

SCHACHTEL, ANNA H. "The Rorschach Test with Young Children." *Am. J. Orthopsychiat.*, 1944, 14, 1-10.

SCHACHTEL, ANNA H., AND LEVI, MARJORIE B. "Character Structure of Day Nursery Children in Wartime as Seen through the Rorschach." *Am. J. Orthopsychiat.*, 1945, 15, 213-22.

SCHACHTEL, ERNEST G. "On Color and Affect; Contributions to an Understanding of the Rorschach Test." *Psychiatry*, 1943, 6, 393-409.

SCHMIDL, FRITZ. The Rorschach test in juvenile delinquency research. *Am. J. Orthopsychiat.*, 1947, 17, 151-160.

SENDER, SADIE & KLOPFER, B. Application of the Rorschach test to child behavior problems as facilitated by a refinement of the scoring method. *Rorschach Res. Exch.*, 1936, No. 1, 1-17.

TROUP, EVELYN. A comparative study by means of the Rorschach method of personality development in twenty pairs of identical twins. *Genet. Psychol. Monogr.*, 1938, 20, 465-556.

VARVEL, W. A. Suggestions toward the experimental validation of the Rorschach test. *Bull. Menninger Clin.*, 1937, 1, 220-226.

VAUGHN, J. & KRUG, OTHILDA. The analytic character of the Rorschach ink blot test. *Am. J. Orthopsychiat.*, 1938, 8, 220-229.

VERNON, P. E. The Rorschach inkblot test. *Brit. J. M. Psychol.*, 1933, 13, 89-118; 179-200; 271-291.

ZUBIN, J. A. Psychometric approach to the evaluation of the Rorschach test. *Psychiatry*, 1941, 4, 547-566.

ZUBIN, J. A. Quantitative approach to measuring regularity of succession in the Rorschach experiment. *Character & Pers.*, 1941, 10, 67-78.

ZUBIN, J. A., CHUTE, E. & VERNIAR, E. Psychometric scales for scoring Rorschach test responses. *Character & Pers.*, 1943, 11, 277-301.

YOUNG, R. A. & HIGGENBOTHAM, S. A. Behavior checks on the Rorschach method. *Am. J. Orthopsychiat.*, 1942, 12, 87-95.

Rorschach Research Exchange. September, 1936, to date.

Thematic Apperception

AMEN, E. W. Individual differences in apperceptive reaction: a study of response of pre-school children to pictures. *Genet. Psychol. Monogr.*, 1941, 23, 319-385.

BALKEN, EVA RUTH. A delineation of schizophrenic language and thought in a test of imagination. *J. Psychol.*, 1943, 16, 239-272.

BALKEN, EVA RUTH & MASSERMAN, J. H. The language of phantasy. III. The language of phantasies of patients with conversion hysteria, anxiety state and obsessive compulsive neuroses. *In* Tomkins, Silvan S. *Contemporary Psychopathology*. Cambridge: Harvard Univ. Press, 1943, pp. 244-253.

BALKEN, EVA RUTH & VANDERVEER, A. H. The clinical application of the Thematic apperception test to neurotic children. *Psychol. Bull.*, 1940, 37, 517. Abstract.

BALKEN, EVA RUTH & VANDERVEER, A. H. The clinical application of a test of imagination to neurotic children. *Am. J. Orthopsychiat.*, 1942, 12, 68-81.

BELLAK, L. An experimental investigation of projection. *Psychol. Bull.*, 1942, 39, 489. Abstract.

BENNETT, GEORGIA. Structural factors related to the substitute value of activities in normal and schizophrenic persons. I. A technique for the investigation of central areas of personality. *Character & Pers.*, 1941, 10, 42-50.

BENNETT, GEORGIA. Some factors related to substitute value at the level of fantasy. *Psychol. Bull.*, 1942, 39, 488. Abstract.

CHRISTENSON, J. A., JR. Clinical application of the Thematic apperception test. *J. Abnorm. & Social Psychol.*, 1943, 38, 104-107.

HARRISON, R. Studies in the use and validity of the Thematic apperception test with mentally disordered patients. II. A quantitative validity study. *Character & Pers.*, 1940, 9, 122-133.

HARRISON, R. Studies in the use and validity of the Thematic apperception test with mentally disordered patients. III. Validation by the method of "blind analysis." *Character & Pers.*, 1940, 9, 134-138.

HARRISON, R. The Thematic apperception and Rorschach methods of personality investigation in clinical practice. *J. Psychol.*, 1943, 15, 49-74.

HARRISON, ROSS & ROTTER, J. B. A note on the reliability of the Thematic apperception test. *J. Abnorm. & Social Psychol.*, 1945, 40, 97-99.

HENRY, WILLIAM F. "The Thematic Apperception Technique in the Study of Culture-Personality Relations." *Genet. Psychol. Monogr.*, 1947, 35: 3-135.

HUTT, M. L. The use of projective methods of personality measurement in army medical installations. *J. Clin. Psychol.*, 1945, 1, 134-140.

KENDIG, I. V. Projective techniques as a psychological tool in diagnosis. *J. Clin. Psychopath. Psychother.*, 1944, 6, 101-110.

KLEIN, G. *Scoring Manual for the Thematic Apperception Test—Research Form*. Army Testing Program. (Mimeographed.)

KUTASH, S. B. Performance of psychopathic defective criminals on the Thematic apperception test. *J. Crim. Psychopath.*, 1943, 5, 319-340.

LASAGA Y TRAVIESO, JOSE I., AND MARTINEZ-ARANGO, CARLOS. "Some Suggestions Concerning the Administration and Interpretation of the TAT." *J. Psychol.*, 1946, 22, 117-63.

LIBBY, W. The imagination of adolescents. *Am. J. Psychol.*, 1908, 19, 249-252.

LOEBLOWITZ-LENNARD, HENRY, AND RIESSMAN, FRANK JR. "Recall in the Thematic Apperception Test: an Experimental Investigation into the Meaning of Recall of Phantasy with Reference to Personality Diagnosis." *J. Pers.*, 1945, 14, 41-46.

MASSERMAN, J. H. & BALKEN, EVA RUTH. The clinical application of phantasy studies. *J. Psychol.*, 1938, 6, 81-88.

MASSERMAN, J. H. & BALKEN, EVA RUTH. The psychoanalytic and psychiatric significance of phantasy. *Psychoanal. Rev.*, 1939, 26, 243-279.

MORGAN, C. D. & MURRAY, H. A. A method for investigating fantasies: the Thematic apperception test. *Arch. Neurol. & Psychiat.*, 1935, 34, 289-306.

MURRAY, H. A. *Manual for the Thematic Apperception Test.* Cambridge, Mass.: Harvard Univ. Press, 1943.

MURRAY, H. A. Techniques for a systematic investigation of fantasy. *J. Psychol.*, 1937, 3, 115-145.

MURRAY, H. A. *Thematic Apperception Test Directions.* Cambridge, Mass.: Harvard Psychological Clinic, 1942. (Mimeographed.)

MURRAY, H. A. & BELLAK, L. *Thematic Apperception Test Blank.* Cambridge, Mass.: Harvard Psychological Clinic, 1941. (Mimeographed.)

RAPAPORT, D. The clinical application of the Thematic apperception test. *Bull. Menninger Clin.*, 1943, 7, 106-113.

RAPAPORT, D. The Thematic apperception test. Qualitative conclusions as to its interpretations. *Psychol. Bull.*, 1942, 39, 592. (Abstract.)

RODNICK, E. H. & KLETANOFF, S. G. Projective reactions to induce frustrations as a measure of social adjustment. *Psychol. Bull.*, 1942, 39, 389. (Abstract.)

ROSENZWEIG, S. & SARASON, S. An experimental study of the triadic hypothesis: reaction to frustration, ego-defense and hypnotizability. I. Correlational approach. II. Thematic apperception approach. *Character & Pers.*, 1942, 11, 1-19, 150-165.

ROTTER, J. B. Studies in the use and validity of the Thematic apperception test with mentally disordered patients. I. Method of analysis and clinical problems. *Character & Pers.*, 1940, 9, 18-34.

ROTTER, JULIAN B. Thematic apperception tests: suggestions for administration and interpretation. *J. Pers.*, 1946, 15, 70-92.

SANFORD, R. N. *Procedure for Scoring the Thematic Apperception Test.* Cambridge: Harvard Psychological Clinic, 1939. (Privately printed.)

SANFORD, R. N. Some quantitative results from the analysis of children's stories. *Psychol. Bull.*, 1941, 38, 749. (Abstract.)

SANFORD, R. N. *Thematic Apperception Test—Directions For Administration and Scoring.* Cambridge: Harvard Psychological Clinic, 1939. (Mimeographed.)

SARASON, S. B. Dreams and Thematic apperception test stories. *J. Abnorm. & Social Psychol.*, 1944, 39, 486-492.

SARASON, S. B. The use of the Thematic apperception test with mentally deficient children. I. A study of high grade girls. *Am. J. Ment. Deficiency*, 1943, 47, 414-421.

SARASON, S. B. & ROSENZWEIG, S. An experimental study of the triadic hypothesis reaction to frustration, ego-defense, and hypnotizability. II. Thematic apperception approach. *Character & Pers.*, 1942, 11, 150-165.

SCHWARTZ, L. A. Social situation pictures in the psychiatric interview. *Am. J. Orthopsychiat.*, 1932, 2, 124-132.

SLUTZ, M. The unique contribution of the Thematic apperception test to a developmental study. *Psychol. Bull.*, 1941, 38, 704. (Abstract.)

SYMONDS, P. M. Adolescent phantasy. *Psychol. Bull.*, 1941, 38, 596. (Abstract.)

SYMONDS, PERCIVAL M. "Inventory of Themes in Adolescent Phantasy." *Am. J. Orthopsychiat.*, 1945, 15, 318-28.

SYMONDS, P. M. Criteria for the selection of pictures for the investigation of adolescent phantasies. *J. Abnorm. & Social Psychol.*, 1939, 34, 271-274.

TOMKINS, S. S. Limits of material obtainable in the single case study by daily administration of the Thematic apperception test. *Psychol. Bull.*, 1942, 39, 490. (Abstract.)

WYATT, F. Advances in the technique of the Thematic apperception test. *Psychol. Bull.*, 1945, 42, 532.
WYATT, F. Formal aspects of the Thematic apperception test. *Psychol. Bull.*, 1942, 39, 491. (Abstract.)

Miscellaneous Projective Techniques

BENDER, LAURETTA. A visual motor Gestalt test and its clinical use. *Res. Monogr. Am. Orthopsychiat. Ass.*, 1938, No. 3.
BENDER, LAURETTA. Group activities on a children's ward as methods of psychotherapy. *Am. J. Psychiat.*, 1937, 93, 1151-1173.
BETTELHEIM, BRUNO. Self-interpretation of fantasy. *Am. J. Orthopsychiat.*, 1947, 17, 80-100.
BIBER, BARBARA, MURPHY, LOIS B., WOODCOCK, LOUISE P., BLACK, IRMA S. *Child Life in School. A Study of a Seven-Year-Old Group.* New York: E. P. Dutton, 1942.
BUHLER, CHARLOTTE. The ball and field test as a help in the diagnosis of emotional difficulties. *Character & Pers.*, 1938, 6, 257-273.
BUHLER, CHARLOTTE & KELLY, G. *The World Test.* New York: Psychological Corporation, 1941.
CATTELL, RAYMOND B. "Projection and the Design of Projective Tests of Personality." *Character & Pers.*, 1944, 12, 175-94.
DERI, SUSAN K. "Description of the Szondi Test; a Projective Technic of Psychological Diagrams." *Am. Psychol.*, 1946, 1, 286.
DESPERT, J. LOUISE. Technical approaches used in the study and treatment of emotional problems in children. Part II. Using a knife under certain conditions. *Psychiat. Quart.*, 1937, 11, 111-130.
DESPERT, J. LOUISE. Technical approaches used in the study and treatment of emotional problems in children. Part I. The story: a form of directed phantasy. *Psychiat. Quart.*, 1936, 10, 619-638.
DESPERT, J. L. & POTTER, H. W. The story, a form of directed phantasy. *Psychiat. Quart.*, 1936, 10, 619-638.
DIAMOND, BERNARD L., AND SCHMALE, HERBERT T. The Mosaic Test. I. An Evaluation of Its Clinical Application." *Am. J. Orthopsychiat.*, 1944, 14, 237-50.
DUBIN, S. S. Verbal attitude scores predicted from responses in a projective technique. *Sociometry*, 1940, 3, 24-48.
FITE, MARY D. Aggressive behavior in young children and children's attitudes toward aggression. *Genet. Psychol. Monogr.*, 1940, 22, 151-319.
FOULDS, G. The child's response to fictional characters and its relationship to personality traits. *Character & Pers.*, 1942, 10, 289-295.
HAGGARD, E. A. A projective technique using comic strip characters. *Character & Pers.*, 1942, 10, 289-295.
HAGGARD, E. A. & SARGENT, HELEN. Use of comic strip characters in diagnosis and therapy. *Psychol. Bull.*, 1941, 38, 714. (Abstract.)
HARROWER, MOLLY R., AND GRINKER, ROY R. "The Stress Tolerance Test." *Psychosom. Med.*, 1946, 8, 3-15.
HELLERSBERG, ELIZABETH F. The Horn-Hellersberg test and adjustment to reality. *Am. J. Orthopsychiat.*, 1945, 15, 690-710.
HOROWITZ, RUTH E. A pictorial method for the study of self-identification in pre-school children. *J. Genet. Psychol.*, 1943, 62, 135-148.
HOROWITZ, RUTH E. Racial aspects of self-identification in nursery school children. *J. Psychol.*, 1939, 7, 91-101.
HOROWITZ, RUTH & HOROWITZ, E. H. Development of social attitudes in children. *Sociometry*, 1938, 1, 301-338.

KELLY, G. A. & BISHOP, F. A projective method of personality investigation. *Psychol. Bull.*, 1942, 39, 599. (Abstract.)

KENT, G. H. & ROSANOFF, A. J. Free-association test. *In* Rosanoff, A. J., *Manual of Psychiatry*. New York: John Wiley & Sons, 1938. Pp. 884-957.

KERR, MADELINE. The validity of the mosaic test. *Am. J. Orthopsychiat.*, 1939, 9, 232-236.

LEVY, J. *The Active Use of Phantasy in Treatment of Children's Behavior Problems.* (Unpublished paper presented at a meeting of the American Psychiatric Association.)

LOEBLOWITZ-LENNARD, HENRY, AND RIESSMAN, FRANK, JR. "A Proposed Projective Attitude Test." *Psychiatry*, 1946, 9, 67-68.

LOWENFELD, MARGARET. The world pictures of children. A method of recording and studying them. *Brit. J. M. Psychol.*, 1939, 18, 65-100.

MARQUIDT, SYBIL. A technique of inquiry into individual personality. *Psychol. Bull.*, 1941, 38, 598. (Abstract.)

MIRA, E. Myokinetic psychodiagnosis: a new technique for exploring the conative trends of personality. *Proc. R. Soc. Med.*, 1940, 33, 9-30.

MURPHY, LOIS B. *Social Behavior and Child Personality.* New York: Columbia Univ. Press, 1937.

PICKFORD, R. W. Imagination and the nonsense syllable: a clinical approach. *Character & Pers.*, 1938, 7, 19-40.

PROSHANSKY, H. M. A projective method for the study of attitudes. *J. Abnorm. & Social Psychol.*, 1943, 38, 393-395.

RAPAPORT, D. The Szondi test. *Bull. Menninger Clin.*, 1941, 5, 33-39.

RODNICK, E. H. & KLEBANOFF, S. G. Projective reactions to induced frustrations as a measure of social adjustment. *Psychol. Bull.*, 1942, 39, 489.

ROHDE, AMANDA R. "Explorations in Personality by the Sentence Completion Method." *J. Applied Psychology*, 1946, 30, 169-81.

ROODY, SARAH I. "The Plot Completion Test." *J. Exper. Educ.*, 1943, 12, 45-47.

ROODY, SARAH I. "Plot Completion Test." *The English Journal*, 1945, 34, 260-65.

ROSENZWEIG, SAUL. *Rosenzweig Picture-Frustration Study.* Pittsburg; the Author (Western State Psychiatric Hospital), 1944.

ROSENZWEIG, SAUL. "The Picture-Association Method and Its Application in a Study of Reactions to Frustration." *J. Pers.*, 1945, 14, 3-23.

ROSENZWEIG, SAUL, AND OTHERS. "Scoring Samples for the Rosenzweig Picture-Frustration Study." *J. Psychol.*, 1946, 21, 45-72.

ROTTER, JULIAN B. "The Incomplete Sentence Test as a Method of Studying Personality." *Am. Psychol.*, 1946, 1, 286.

SANFORD, R. N. Some quantitative results from the analysis of children's stories. *Psychol. Bull.*, 1941, 38, 749.

SARGENT, HELEN. An experimental application of projective principles in a paper and pencil personality test. *Psychol. Monogr.*, 1944, 57, No. 5, 1-57.

SCHWARTZ, L. A. *Social-situation Pictures in the Psychiatric Interview.* Paper presented at the meeting of the American Orthopsychiatric Association, 1931.

STERN, W. Cloud pictures: a new method for testing imagination. *Character & Pers.*, 1938, 6, 132-146.

TUDDENHEIM, R. The reputation test as a projective technique. *Psychol. Bull.*, 1931, 38, 749. (Abstract.)

WERTHAM, F. & GOLDEN, LILI. A differential diagnostic method of interpreting mosaic and colored block designs. *Am. J. Orthopsychiat.*, 1941, 98, 124-131.

WOLFENSTEIN, MARTHA. "Reality Principles in Story Preferences of Neurotics and Psychotics." *Character & Pers.*, 1944, 13, 135-51.

SECTION III. SUPPLEMENTARY REFERENCES

ABRAMSON, H. A., *et al.* Non-projective personality tests. *Ann. N. Y. Acad. Sci.*, 1946, 46, 531-678.

ALLPORT, F. H. Teleonomic description in the study of personality. *Character & Pers.*, 1937, 5, 202-214.

ALLPORT, G. W. Personal documents in psychological science. *Soc. Sci. Res. Coun. Monogr.*, 1942, No. 49.

ALLPORT, G. W. *Personality: A Psychological Interpretation.* New York: Holt, 1937.

ALLPORT, G. W. The psychologist's frame of reference. *Psychol. Bull.*, 1940, 37, 1-28.

ALLPORT, G. W., & VERNON, P. E. *Studies in Expressive Movement.* New York: Macmillan, 1933.

BALDWIN, A. L. The statistical analysis of the structure of a single personality. *Psychol. Bull.*, 1940, 37, 518-519. (Abstract.)

BALKEN, EVA RUTH. Psychological researches in schizophrenic language and thought. *J. Psychol.*, 1943, 16, 153-176.

BARKER, R. G. The effect of frustration upon cognitive ability. *Character & Pers.*, 1938, 7, 145-150.

BARKER, R. G., DEMBO, T. & LEWIN, K. Experiments in frustration and regression studies in topological and vector psychology. *Iowa Child Wel. Res. St. Monogr.*, 1939.

BARTLETT, F. C. An experimental study of some problems of perceiving and imagining. *Brit. J. Psychol.*, 1916, 8, 222-266.

BENDER, LAURETTA, KEISER, S. & SCHILDER, P. Studies in aggressiveness. *Genet. Psychol. Monogr.*, 1936, 18, 357-564.

BLEULER, E. Upon the significance of association experiments. *In* Jung, C. G. *Studies in Word Association.* (Trans. by M. R. Eder.) New York: Moffatt Yard & Co., 1919.

BOOTH, G. C. Personality and chronic arthritis. *J. Nerv. & Ment. Dis.*, 1937, 85, 637-662.

BOYNTON, P. L. & WALSWORTH, B. M. Emotionality test scores for delinquent and non-delinquent girls. *J. Abnorm. & Social Psychol.*, 1943, 38, 87-93.

BRITTAIN, H. L. A study of imagination. *Ped. Sem.*, 1907, 14, 137-207.

BROWN, J. F. *Psychodynamics of Abnormal Behavior.* New York: McGraw Hill, 1940.

CAMERON, N. Individual and social factors in the development of graphic symbolization. *J. Psychol.*, 1938, 5, 165-183.

CAMERON, N. Functional immaturity in the symbolization of scientifically trained adults. *J. Psychol.*, 1938, 6, 161-175.

CAMERON, N. Reasoning, regression, and communication in schizophrenics. *Psychol. Monogr.*, 1938, 50, 1-34.

CAMERON, N. Deterioration and regression in schizophrenic thinking. *J. Abnorm. & Social Psychol.*, 1939, 34, 265-270.

CARTWRIGHT, D. & FRENCH, J. R. R., JR. The reliability of life history studies. *Character & Pers.*, 1939, 8, 110-119.

CLARK, L. P. The phantasy method of analyzing narcissistic neuroses. *Med. J. Rec.*, 1926, 123, 154-158.

CONKLIN, E. S. The foster child phantasy. *Am. J. Psychol.*, 1920, 32, 59-76.

CROSSLAND, H. R. The psychological method of word-association. *Univ. Oregon Psychol. Ser.*, 1929.

DAVIS, F. P., JR. *Diagnostic Methods in Clinical Psychology.* Unpublished doctoral dissertation. Univ. Texas, 1943.

DUFF, I. F. A psychoanalytic study of a fantasy of St. Therese de l'enfant Jesus. *Brit. J. M. Psychol.,* 1926, 5, 345-353.

FREUD, ANNA. *The Ego and the Mechanisms of Defense.* (Trans. by C. Baines.) London: Hogarth, 1937.

FREUD, S. *General Introduction to Psychoanalysis.* New York: Boni & Liveright, 1920.

GERARD, MARGARET W. Case for discussion at the 1938 symposium. *Am. J. Orthopsychiat.,* 1938, 8, 1-18.

GREEN, G. H. *The Daydream. A Study in Development.* London: Univ. London Press, 1923.

GRIFFITHS, R. A. *A Study of Imagination in Early Childhood, and its Function in Early Development.* London: Kegan Paul, 1935.

GRIFFITHS, R. A. *Imagination in Young Children.* London: Kegan Paul, 1936.

HALL, G. S. Notes on cloud fancies. *Ped. Sem.,* 1903, 10, 96-100.

HANFMANN, EUGENIA. Social structure of a group of kindergarten children. *Am. J. Orthopsychiat.,* 1935, 5, 407-410.

HANFMANN, EUGENIA. Disturbances in concept formation in schizophrenia. *Arch. Neurol. & Psychiat.,* 1938, 40, 1276-1282.

HANFMANN, EUGENIA. Analysis of the thinking disorder in a case of schizophrenia. *Arch. Neurol. & Psychiat.,* 1939, 41, 568-579.

HANFMANN, EUGENIA & KASANIN, J. A method for the study of concept formation. *J. Psychol.,* 1937, 3, 521-540.

HARTSHORNE, HUGH. A psychological approach to reality. *Soc. Sci.,* 1936, 11, 312-321.

HARVEY, N. A. Imaginary playmates and other mental phenomena of children. Ypsilanti, Mich., State Normal College, 1918.

HERTZ, MARGUERITE R., ELLIS, ALBERT, AND SYMONDS, PERCIVAL P. "Research Methods and Other Propective Techniques." *Rev. Educ. Res.,* 1947. 17.

HULL, C. L. & LUGOFF, L. S. Complex signs in diagnostic free association. *J. Exper. Psychol.,* 1941, 4, 111-136.

JAENSCH, E. R. *Eidetic Imagery and Typological Methods of Investigation.* New York: Harcourt Brace, 1930.

JOHNSON, W. The quantitative study of language behavior. *Psychol. Bull.,* 1931, 38, 528. (Abstract.)

JOHNSON, W., FAIRBANKS, HELEN, MANN, MARY B., & CHOTLOS, J. W. Studies in language behavior. *Psychol. Monogr.,* 1944, 56, No. 2.

JOHNSON, W. *Language and Speech Hygiene.* Chicago: Institute of General Semantics, 1939.

JUNG, C. G. The association method. *Am. J. Psychol.,* 1910, 21, 219-269.

JUNG, C. G. *Studies in Word Association.* (Trans. by M. D. Eder.) New York: Moffatt Yard & Co., 1919.

KANTOR, J. H. Current trends in psychological theory. *Psychol. Bull.,* 1941, 38, 29-61.

KASANIN, J., & HANFMANN, EUGENIA. An experimental study of concept formation in schizophrenia: I. Quantitative analysis of the results. *Am. J. Psychiat.,* 1938, 95, 35-48.

KENT, GRACE H. & ROSANOFF, A. The study of association in insanity. *Am. J. Insan.,* 1910, 67, 37-96.

KLUVER, H. The eidetic child. *In Handbook of Child Psychology.* Worcester. Mass.: Clark Univ. Press, 1931.

LEHRMANN, P. R. Phantasy in neurotic behavior. *Med. J. Rec.* 1927, 126, 342-344.

LEHRMANN, P. R. The phantasy of not belonging to one's family. *Arch. Neurol. & Psychiat.*, 1927, 18, 1015-1025.

LEWIN, K. *A Dynamic Theory of Personality.* New York: McGraw Hill, 1935.

LEWIN, K. Environmental forces. *In* Murchison, C., *Handbook of Child Psychology.* Worcester, Mass.: Clark Univ. Press, 1933.

LEWIN, K. *Principles of Topological Psychology.* New York: McGraw-Hill, 1936.

LEWIN, K. Psychoanalysis and topological psychology. *Bull. Menninger Clin.*, 1937, 1, 202-211.

LLOYD, WILMA. Some aspects of language as significant of personality. *Psychol. Bull.*, 1941, 38, 747. (Abstract.)

LOWENFELD, V. *The Nature of Creative Activity.* London, Kegan Paul, 1938.

MacCURDY, J. Phantasy of the mother's body in the Hephaestus myth and a novel by Bulwer-Lytton. *Psychoanal. Rev.*, 1920, 7, 295. (Abstract.)

MacKINNON, DONALD W. Some problems of assessment. *Tr. N. Y. Acad. Cci.*, 1947, 9, 171-205.

MARTIN, ALEXANDER REID. A study of parental attitudes and their influence upon personality development. *Educ.*, 1943, 1-13.

MASLOW, A. H. Dynamics of personality organization. *Psychol. Rev.*, 1943, 50, 514-539, 541-558.

MEAD, MARGARET. "The Concept of Culture and the Psychosomatic Approach." *Psychiatry*, 1947. 10: 57-76.

MORENO, J. L. Creativity and cultural conserves—with special reference to musical expression. *Sociometry*, 1939, 2, 1-36.

MORENO, J. L. & JENNINGS, H. Spontaneity training, a method of personality development. *Sociometric Rev.*, 1936.

MORENO, J. L. Who shall survive? *Nerv. Ment. Dis. Monogr.*, 1934, No. 58.

MUNROE, RUTH L. "Three Diagnostic Methods Applied to Sally." *J. Abnorm. & Social Psychol.*, 1945, 40, 215-27.

MUNROE, RUTH L.; LEWINSOHN, THEA S.; AND WAEHNER, TRUDE S. "A Comparison of Three Projective Methods." *Character & Pers.*, 1944, 13, 1-21.

MURRAY, H. A. & MacKINNON, DONALD W. Assessment of OSS personnel. *J. Consult. Psychol.*, 1946, 10, 46-80.

NEWMAN, S. Personal symbolism in language patterns. *Psychiatry*, 1939, 2, 177-183.

NEWMAN, S. & MATHER, V. G. Analysis of spoken language of patients with affective disorders. *Am. J. Psychiat.*, 1938, 94, 913-942.

PLANT, J. S. Personality and the culture pattern. *J. Soc. Philos.*, 1938, 3.

PORTER, E. L. H. Factors in the fluctuation of fifteen ambiguous phenomena. *Psychol. Rec.*, 1937, 2, 231-253.

RAUTMAN, A. L. & BROWER, E. War themes in children's stories. *J. Psychol.*, 1945, 19, 191-202.

ROBINSON, E. E. The compensatory function of make-believe play. *Psychol. Rev.*, 1920, 27, 434-438.

ROSANOFF, A. J. *The Free Association Test.* (Reprinted from *Manual of Psychiatry*.) New York, Wiley, 1927.

SANFORD, F. H. Speech and personality. *Psychol. Bull.*, 1942, 39, 811-845.

SANFORD, F. H. Speech and personality: a comparative case study. *Character & Pers.*, 1942, 10, 169-198.

SANFORD, R. NEVITT. Psychological approaches to the young delinquent. *J. Consult. Psychol.*, 1943, 7, 223-229.

SANFORD, R. NEVITT, AND COBB, ELIZABETH A. "Studies of Personality and the Environment." Physique, Personality, and Scholarship. Monographs of the Society for Research in Child Development. Vol. 8, No. 1 (Serial No. 34) Washington, D. C.: *Soc. for Res. in Child Devel.*, 1943. Part III, p. 125-361.

SAPIR, E. The emergence of the concept of personality in a study of culture. *J. Soc. Psychol.*, 1934, 5, 408-415.

SCHACHTEL, ERNEST G. "On Memory and Childhood Amnesia." *Psychiatry* 1947. 10, 1-26.

SEASHORE, R. H. *Fields of Psychology.* An experimental approach. (Chap. 40. Convergent trends in psychological theory.) New York: Holt, 1942.

SOUTHARD, E. E. On the application of grammatical categories to the analysis of delusions. *Phil. Rev., N. Y.*, 1916, 25, 424-455.

SYMONDS, PERCIVAL M. AND KRUGMAN, MORRIS. "Projective Methods in the Study of Personality." *Rev. Educ. Res.*, 14: 81-98; February 1944.

SYMONDS, P. M. *Diagnosing Personality and Conduct.* New York: Century, 1931.

THURSTONE, L. L. The stimulus response fallacy. *Psychol. Rev.*, 1922, 30, No. 5.

VARENDONCK, J. *The Psychology of Daydreams.* London: Allen & Unwin, 1921.

VERNON, M. D. The relation of cognition and phantasy in children. *Brit. J. Psychol.*, 1940, 31, 1-19.

VERNON, P. E. The matching method applied to investigations of personality. *Psychol. Bull.*, 1936, 33, 149-177.

VIGOTSKY, L. L. Thought and speech. (Trans. by Drs. Helen Kogan, Eugenia Hanfmann, and Jacob Kasanin.) *Psychiatry*, 1939, 8, 29-54.

WELLS, F. L. & WOODWORTH, R. S. Association tests. *Psychol. Rev. Monogr. Sup.*, 1911, No. 57.

WERNER, H. William Stern's personalistics and psychology of personality. *Character & Pers.*, 1938, 7, 109-125.

WHITE, ROBERT W. "Interpretation of Imaginative Production." *Personality and Behavior Disorders.* New York: Ronald Press, 1944. Vol. I, p. 214-51.

Further elaboration and discussions of some of the concepts and assumptions offered in this lecture will be found in the following papers by the author. Some of these papers will appear early in 1948 in a volume entitled, *Society as the Patient.* Rutgers University Press, 1948.

FRANK, L. K. The management of tensions. *Am. J. Sociol.*, 1928, 33, 705-736.

FRANK, L. K. Physiological tensions and social structure. *Publ. Am. Sociological Soc.*, 1928, 22, 74-82.

FRANK, L. K. Personality and rank order. *Am. J. Sociol.*, 1929, 35, 177-186.

FRANK, L. K. The concept of inviolability in culture. *Am. J. Sociol.*, 1931, 36, 607-615.

FRANK, L. K. Causation: An episode in the history of thought. *J. Philosophy*, 1934, 31, 421-428.

FRANK, L. K. Structure, function and growth. *Philosophy of Science*, 1935, 2, 210-235.

FRANK, L. K. The fundamental needs of the child. *Ment. Hyg.*, 1938, 22, 353-379.

FRANK, L. K. Time perspectives. *J. Social Philosophy*, 1939, 4, 293-312.

FRANK, L. K. Cultural coercion and individual distortion. *Psychiatry*, 1939, 2, 11-27.

FRANK, L. K. The reorientation of education to the promotion of mental hygiene. *Ment. Hyg.*, 1939, 23, 529-543.

FRANK, L. K. The family as cultural agent. *Living,* 1940, 2, 16-19.

FRANK, L. K. Science and culture. *Scientific Monthly,* 1940, 50, 491-497.

FRANK, L. K. Freedom for the personality. *Psychiatry,* 1940, 3, 341-349.

FRANK, L. K. Freud's influence on western thinking and culture. *Am. J. Orthopsychiat.,* 1940, 10, 880-882.

FRANK, L. K. Social order and psychiatry. *Am. J. Orthopsychiat.,* 1941, 11, 620-627.

FRANK, L. K. Adolescence and public health. *Am. J. Pub. Health,* 1941, 31, 1943.

FRANK, L. K. Research in orthopsychiatry. *Am. J. Orthopsychiat.,* 1943, 13 (2), 244-248.

FRANK, L. K. Man's multidimensional environment. *Scientific Monthly,* 1943, 56, 344-358.

FRANK, L. K. Research in child psychology, history and prospect. Chapter I, in: *Child Behavior and Development.* McGraw-Hill: New York, 1943.

FRANK, L. K. Opportunities and obligations of orthopsychiatry. *Am. J. Orthopsychiat.,* 1943, 13 (4).

FRANK, L. K. The Emergence of Personality. *Tr. N. Y. Acad. Sci.,* 1944, Ser. II, Vol. 6, No. 5, 149-156.

FRANK, L K. Gerontology. *J. Gerontology,* 1946, I, No. 1, 1-12.

THIS BOOK

PROJECTIVE METHODS

by

LAWRENCE K. FRANK

was set and printed by The Anthoensen Press of Portland, Maine; and bound by the Pantagraph Printing and Stationery Company of Bloomington, Illinois. The type face is Linotype Janson, set 12 point on 13 point. The type page is 25 x 43 picas. The text paper is white wove, Tru-Colour. The cover is No. 25, Black Pajco Lepide, embossing pattern No. 32, TT.

With THOMAS BOOKS *careful attention is given to all details of manufacturing and design. It is the publisher's desire to present books that are satisfactory as to their physical qualities and artistic possibilities and appropriate for their particular use.* THOMAS BOOKS *will be true to those laws of quality that assure a good name and good will.*